A prac
introduc
Microsoft Office 2000

i

Other Titles of Interest

BP440   Explaining Microsoft Money 97

BP441   Creating Web Pages using Microsoft Office 97

BP442   Explaining Microsoft Publisher 97

BP452   A Practical Introduction to Microsoft Office 97

BP461   Using FrontPage 98

BP476   Microsoft PowerPoint 2000 Explained

BP477   Using Microsoft FrontPage 2000

BP480   A Practical Introduction to Sage Line 50

BP482   Sage Instant Accounting 2000

BP490   Web Pages using Microsoft Office 2000

A practical introduction to Microsoft Office 2000

David Weale

Bernard Babani (Publishing) Ltd
The Grampians
Shepherds Bush Road
London W6 7NF
England

Please Note

Although every care has been taken with the production of this book to ensure that any instructions or any of the other contents operate in a correct and safe manner, the Author and the Publishers do not accept any responsibility for any failure, damage, or loss caused by following the said contents. The Author and Publisher do not take any responsibility for errors or omissions.

The Author and Publisher make no warranty or representation, either express or implied, with respect to the contents of this book, its quality, merchantability or fitness for a particular purpose.

The Author and Publisher will not be liable to the purchaser or to any other person or legal entity with respect to any liability, loss or damage (whether direct, indirect, special, incidental or consequential) caused or alleged to be caused directly or indirectly by this book.

The book is sold as is, without any warranty of any kind, either expressed or implied, respecting the contents, including but not limited to implied warranties regarding the book's quality, performance, correctness or fitness for any particular purpose.

No part of this book may be reproduced or copied by any means whatever without written permission of the publisher.

© 2000 BERNARD BABANI (publishing) LTD

First Published - September 2000

British Library Cataloguing in Publication Data

A catalogue record for this book is available from the British Library

ISBN 0 85934 492 4

Cover Design by Gregor Arthur

Printed and bound in Great Britain by Guernsey Press

Preface

Welcome to Microsoft® Office 2000.

I wrote this book to help you in learning how to use Office 2000 practically. It is intended to explain the program in a way that I hope you will find useful, and that you will learn by doing.

Each section of the book covers a different aspect of the program and contains various hints and tips which I have found useful and may enhance your work.

By working through the material and practising it, you will build up an expertise in the use of the applications.

The text is written both for the new user and for the more experienced person who wants an easy to follow reference.

Please note that you should know how to use the basic techniques of Microsoft® Windows® 98; if you do not, there are many excellent texts on the subject.

I hope you learn from this book and have fun doing so.

Best wishes,

David Weale September 2000

Trademarks

Microsoft®, MS-DOS, PowerPoint®, and Windows® are registered trademarks or trademarks of Microsoft® Corporation.

All other trademarks are the registered and legally protected trademarks of the companies who make the products. There is no intent to use the trademarks generally and readers should investigate ownership of a trademark before using it for any purpose.

Dedication

To those who have passed before.

About the author

David Weale is a Fellow of the Institute of Chartered Accountants and has worked in both private and public practice. At present, he is a lecturer in business computing.

Contents

Word 1
  Viewing the screen...2
  Text entry 3
    Opening files and adding text... 6
    Editing text 8
    Previewing your work 9
    Alignment... 10
    Formatting 13
    Format Painter 15
    Line Spacing... 16
    Page Breaks 17
    Widows and Orphans.. 18
    Moving text (cut & paste)... 20
    Borders 22
    Indenting... 25
    Headers & Footers.. 27
  Printing...30
    Numbering paragraphs 31
    Bullets... 32
    Search and replace... 33
  Inserting clipart 34
    Word Art... 37
    Using the Drawing Tools... 39
    Counting the number of words 39
    Page Setup 40
    Adding Footnotes 42
    Changing Case.. 44
    Creating columns.. 45
    Tables 47
    Using Tab settings 52
    Importing text 53
  Text Styles 54
    Altering styles.. 56
  TOC (table of contents) 58
  Inserting fields 60
  Templates...62

Exercise 63
Mailmerging 64
Customising the toolbars 70
Excel **73**
Starting off 74
   Moving around the worksheet 75
   Entering text or numbers 75
Saving your work 76
   Copying cells 77
   Aligning cells.. 77
Entering formulae 79
   Inserting rows and columns 81
   Centring text (across columns) 81
   Altering the fonts 82
Borders and patterns 83
   Viewing the formula 85
Page Setup 86
   Previewing the worksheet 89
   Printing your worksheet 89
   Closing the file 90
   Starting a new file 90
   A new exercise 90
   Altering column (or row) width 91
   Entering formulae 92
   Sorting the data 93
   AutoFormat 96
   Another new exercise 97
Arithmetic calculations 98
   Formatting numbered cells 99
   Cell alignment 100
   The next exercise 103
Functions 104
   Conditional Function 107
   Example 107
   Exercise 109
   Pivot Tables 110
   Lookup 114
   Absolute referencing 117
   Freezing panes 119

Charts and Graphs...120
   The Chart Wizard 120
   Altering the look of the chart... 125
   Altering the text font & alignment 126
   Altering the chart... 128
   Headers & Footers 129
   Changing the names of the worksheets 130
   Adding legends and X-series labels.............................. 131
   Changing the X-series labels 132
   Changing the legend descriptions................................. 132
   Altering the position of the X-series labels 135
   Altering the Y-axis scale 138
   Reorganising the series order 140
   Practice 141
   Adding text boxes and arrows 142
Pie Charts 143
Pictograms..145
Pasting charts and worksheets into Word 147
   Worksheets (data) 147
   Charts.. 148
   Linking the Word and Excel files................................... 148
   Practice 149

PowerPoint...151
Starting off 152
Creating a new presentation..153
   Entering Text 156
Saving your work...159
Text editing 159
   Transitions 165
   Animations 167
Looking at your Slides 168
   Slide Sorter 168
   Printing the slides 168
   Slide Designs 170
Adding Graphics 172
   Clipart... 172
   WordArt.. 174
   Organisation Charts 177

Borders/Arrows 181
Adding sounds (and movies) 183
Altering Slides 186
Master Slides 186
Running slide shows automatically 188
Setting timings.. 189

Access 191
What is a database...192
The structure 193
Flat-form databases... 194
Relational databases 194
Beginnings 195
Adding data to a database... 201
Sorting the data... 202
Applying Filters... 204
Forms... 205
Reports... 209
Customising the report layout....................................... 213
Practice 215
Relationships between tables... 217
Creating the relationship... 217
Queries 221
Creating a report from a query 223
Extracting data from a database.................................... 225

Appendices 229
The Standard Buttons...230
Help..231
The Office Assistant 232
The Options button 233
The Search button 233
Using the Show button 235
Contents 235
Answer Wizard 236
Index 237
Office on the Web.. 238
Detect and Repair 238
About Microsoft (Access) 238
Index 239

Word

Viewing the screen

There are several different ways of looking at your document.

For the purpose of this text, the two you will be using are **Normal** (this is the default) and **Print Layout** (this displays the page as it would appear when printed, e.g. with each page shown separately).

Examples are shown below, **Normal** view first, followed by **Print Layout** view.

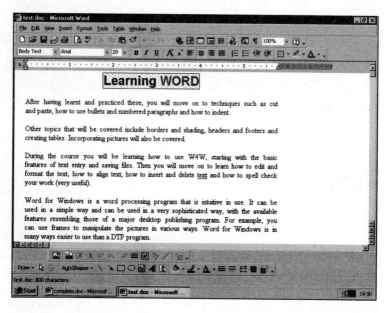

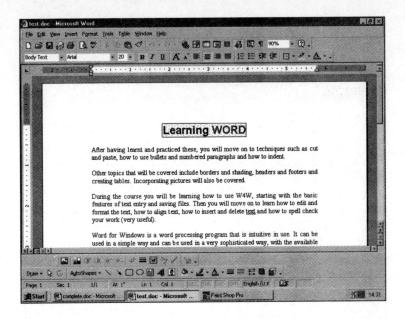

To alter the view, pull down the **View** menu and then select the view you want.

Text entry

Please type in the text (shown on the next page).

Do **not** use the **return** key until the end of the paragraph.

See how any spelling mistakes are identified with red underlining and grammatical errors with green underlining. Do **not** correct them at present.

You should leave **only** a single space after commas or full stops.

Word for Windows is a word processing program that is intuitive in use. It can be used in a simple way and can be used in a very sophisticated way, with the available features resembling those of a major desktop publishing program. Word for Windows is in many ways easier to use than a DTP program especially for the non-professional.

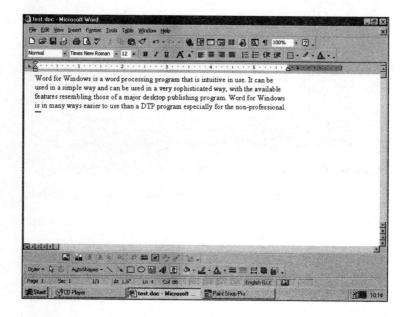

Click the **Save** button (on the toolbar), the **Save As** dialog box will be displayed, call your file TEST and save it in a folder of your choice.

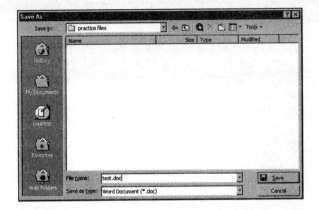

Close the file (pull down the **File** menu and select **Close**).

Opening files and adding text

To open the file, click the **Open** button and then select the file you want to open and click on **Open** (or double-click the filename).

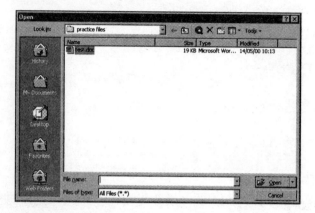

Move the cursor to the end of the text (**Ctrl** and **End** - hold the **Ctrl** key down while pressing the second key).

Press the **return** key twice to create a blank line and then enter the new text (you should end up with two paragraphs with a blank line between them).

During the course, you will be learning how to use W4W, starting with the basic features of text entry and saving files. Then you will move on to learn how to edit and format the text, how to align text, how to insert and delete text, and how to spell check your work (very useful).

Save the file by clicking on the **Save** button on the toolbar and then enter the following text in the same way.

After having learnt and practised these, you will move on to techniques such as cut and paste, how to use bullets and numbered paragraphs and how to indent.

Other topics that will be covered include borders and shading, headers and footers and creating tables. Incorporating pictures will also be covered.

You should now have four separate paragraphs.

Save the file.

Your screen should look similar to this.

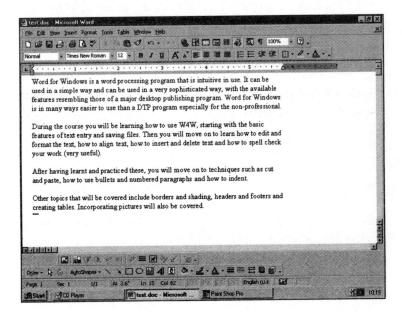

Editing text

You may want to edit (alter) the text.

To begin this, move the cursor to the end of the second sentence (first paragraph) and enter the following as a new sentence (spelt as shown - some of the mistakes may be automatically corrected). The rest of the text will move to make space.

Ffor exampel you cann use frames to manippulate the picturs in various ways.

If you need to delete text, click the mouse at the start or end of the words and (keeping the mouse button depressed) move the mouse across the words until all are highlighted and then press the **Delete** key on the keyboard.

Move the cursor to the end of the first paragraph.

Delete the last four words (so that the final word within the paragraph is program).

Save the file.

Previewing your work

Modern word processing programs have a preview feature that lets you see how the text will look **before** printing it out. This saves both time and paper.

Click on the **Preview** button on the toolbar and you will see the text displayed, as it will be printed out.

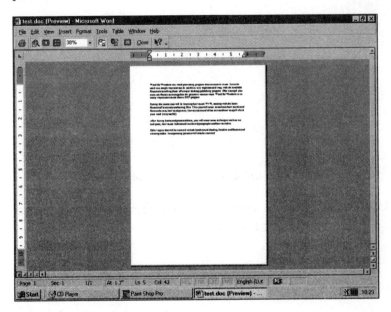

Note the **Multiple Page** button and the **Zoom** button. By clicking on these, you can alter the number of pages and size of the page(s).

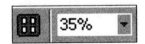

There is also a very useful feature called **Shrink to Fit** that will attempt to fit the file onto one fewer pages. To use this, click the button along the toolbar of the **preview** screen.

Click on the **Close** button to return to the previous screen.

Alignment

Position the cursor within the first paragraph and then click on the **Justify** button. Notice the effect, the right-hand margin will be straight.

Position the cursor within the second paragraph and click on the **Center** button.

Position the cursor within the third paragraph and click on the **Align Right** button. Look at how the text is laid out on the page by previewing it.

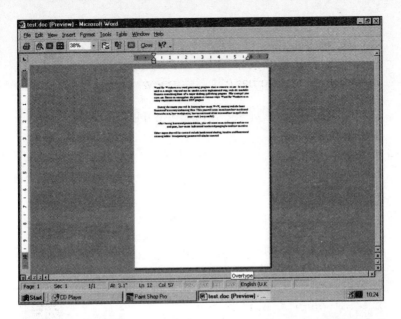

Highlight all the text (by clicking the mouse at the start of the text and holding down the mouse button, drag the mouse over the text, letting go **only** when the required area is highlighted).

Click on the **Justify** button, and look at how the text is laid out on the page by previewing it (the right-hand margin of the text should be straight) as you can see from the illustration.

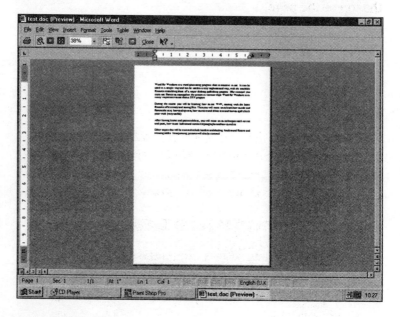

Save the file.

Formatting

Position the cursor at the very start of the page (**Ctrl Home**) and use the **return** key to create two blank lines at the top of the page.

Move the cursor to the very top and enter the following title.

Learning WORD

Highlight the title then click on the **Bold** button on the toolbar, and then highlight (the word) WORD and pull down the **Format** menu, select **Font** then **Font color** and colour it red.

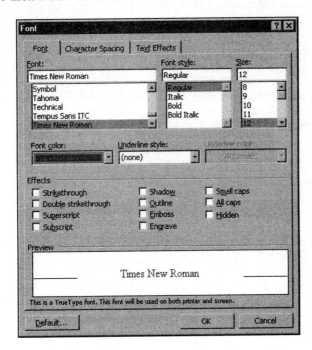

Alternatively, you can click the arrow to the right of the **Font Color** button to select a colour.

There is a choice of **Serif** or **Sans Serif** fonts.

Serif fonts e.g. **Times New Roman** have a serif or line running along the bottom of certain characters (the body text of this book uses Times New Roman).

Sans Serif fonts do not have a serif and tend to be used for titles and headings. An example of this type of font is **Arial**.

With all of the title highlighted, click on the **Font** display button on the toolbar (specifically the arrow to the right of the font name) and from the resulting list of fonts choose Arial.

Do the same with the **Font Size**, this time selecting 20.

The title should now stand out from the text.

Finally, centre the title.

Format Painter

You can copy formats using the **Format Painter** button on the toolbar.

This is a very powerful tool, to use it, click the mouse on the text you want to copy the format from, click the button and then click and drag the mouse over the text you want to copy the formatting to.

Practise this and then use the **Undo** button to remove the changes.

Line Spacing

Click within the last paragraph and while holding down the **Ctrl** key press the number **2** key (above the QWERTY keys). This will double-space the paragraph.

Repeat this process, only this time use **Ctrl** and the number **1** key, the text should revert to single-line spacing.

Your file should look like this when previewed.

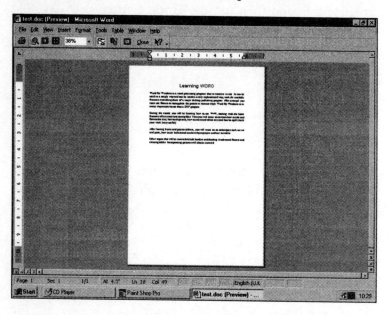

Save the file (with the same name) and close it.

Page Breaks

Open the file TEST.

WORD automatically sets page breaks (i.e. where a new page starts). You may want to alter these, for example, the program may put a page break in the middle of a paragraph (it is normally thought poor layout to have one or two lines of a paragraph ending up on the preceding or following page).

To set **page breaks** position the cursor where you want the page break to appear and then press the **return** key *while* holding down the **Ctrl** key. You will see a dotted line appear across the page, this shows a page break.

To remove a page break, position the cursor on the dotted line and press the **Delete** key.

Put a page break between paragraph one and paragraph two and another between paragraph two and paragraph three.

Move the cursor to the top of the file and preview the file. You should see that it now extends to three separate pages.

Remove the page breaks and preview the file again to make sure that it is now all on one page. Close the file (**File Close**) **without** saving the changes.

Widows and Orphans

A widow or orphan is a line of text, which appears on a page, the remainder of the paragraph appearing on the previous/next page.

To avoid having widows or orphans, select the paragraphs and pull down the **Format** menu, click **Paragraph**, and then click the **Line and Page Breaks** tab. Select the **Widow/Orphan control** check box.

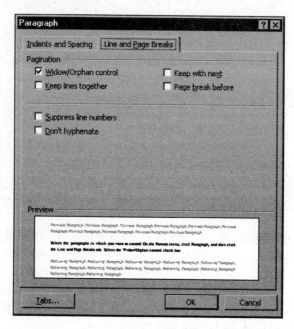

There is a **Keep lines together** option, which works in a similar way and will keep highlighted text together on the same page.

Spell and grammar checking

Inevitably, you will type some words incorrectly and having access to a spell checker is very useful.

Open the file (TEST) and make sure that the cursor is at the top of the page.

Click on the spell-checking button.

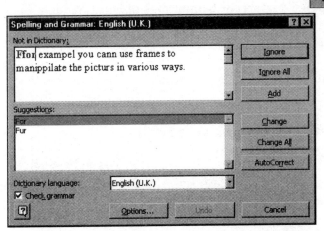

You can **Add** to the dictionary (inevitably the dictionary is finite in size and a word may be correct but be identified by the spell checker since it is not in the dictionary).

Change the words as necessary by clicking on the **Change** button and then **Save** the file.

This version of WORD also checks your grammar!

Moving text (cut & paste)

After entering the data, you may want to move some of the text around.

There are several ways to do this; the one you are going to use is the standard Windows technique of **Cut & Paste**.

This technique is common to all Windows applications and can be used both within one application and between applications (for example to copy a picture from PowerPoint® to W4W).

Highlight the second paragraph.

Click on the **Cut** button and the text will be cut from your document (it is held in the Windows **Clipboard**).

Move the cursor to the end of the document (**returning** if necessary to create a blank line).

Click on the **Paste** button and the paragraph you cut will reappear.

If there is too much or too little space between the paragraphs, use the **return** or **Delete** keys as necessary.

Now cut the first paragraph and paste it below the last (to practise the technique).

Preview the file and then **Save** it.

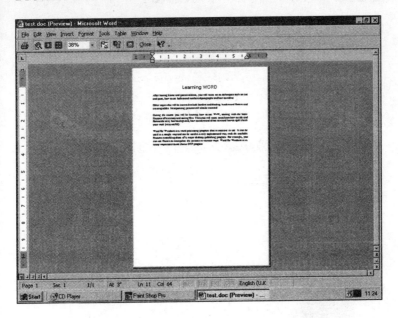

Borders

One way of making text stand out is to place a border around it; this border can be shaded (filled with a pattern) if you wish.

Highlight the third paragraph, pull down the **Format** menu, and select **Borders and Shading**.

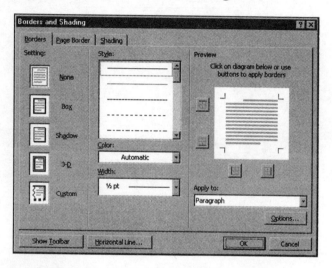

Choose the border **Style**, **Color** and **Width** you want, make sure that the **Apply To** box shows the word **Paragraph**. Finally, click on **Box** and then on **OK**

You should now have a border around the text.

Repeat this operation for the first paragraph using a different type of border.

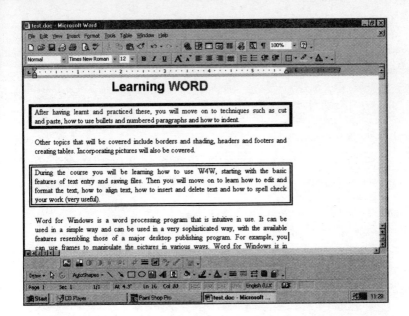

Now highlight each bordered paragraph (in turn), selecting **Format**, followed by **Borders and Shading**. Make sure that **Paragraph** is selected in the **Apply To** box and then select **None**. This will remove the borders.

Finally place a shadowed border around the title; check that you have highlighted just the title and that the **Apply To** box displays **Text** and this time also select **Shading**. Choose a suitable **Pattern Style** and **Color** (again ensuring that the **Apply To** box shows **Text**).

Preview the result and **Save** the file.

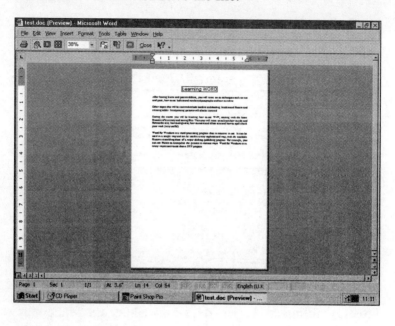

Indenting

Another method of making text stand out is to use a technique called Indents.

Highlight the third paragraph and then pull down the **Format** menu. Select **Paragraph** and then **Indents and Spacing**; enter the figures 2" for both left and right indents within the dialog box that appears.

To alter the measurements from centimetres to inches, pull down the **Tools** menu and select **Options** and then **General**. You will see the **Measurement units** at the bottom of this box.

Indent the first paragraph by 3" (left indent only).

Preview the file and you will see the way the indented paragraphs stand out.

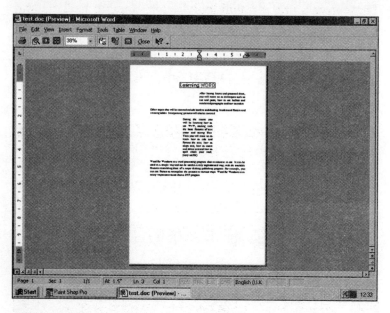

Remove the paragraph indents for paragraphs one and three by highlighting the paragraphs and resetting the left and right indents to zero (remember you can use the **F4** key to repeat formatting).

Save the file.

Headers & Footers

These give a professional look to a document; headers and footers are text (or pictures) that appear at the top or bottom of each page.

Pull down the **View** menu and select **Header and Footer**. The toolbar will be displayed.

Switch to the **Footer**, by clicking on the **Switch** button, and you will see the screen alter so that a footer section appears in the lower part of the screen.

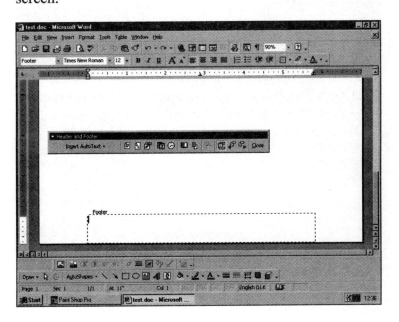

Enter the page number by clicking on the **Insert Page Number** button.

Highlight the page number; change the font to italic and two points smaller than the rest of the text. Finally, right align it.

Close the footer window and preview your text, you should see the footer at the bottom of the page.

Add your name as a header; format it to italic, two points smaller than the text and left aligned.

Preview and save the file.

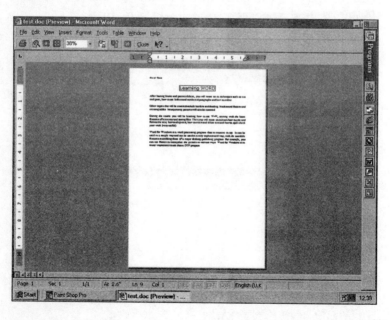

You can add any text, date, or symbols to the header or footer.

To add a date, pull down the **Insert** menus and select **Date and Time** (this gives more choice than using the **Date** button in the toolbar).

To insert a symbol (for example a copyright symbol ©), pull down the **Insert** menu and select **Symbol**).

Printing

You have learnt how to preview your work, printing it out is almost as simple.

You have two options when you print.

Use the **Print** button on the toolbar. This will print to the default printer.

Pull down the **File** menu and then **Print**. This option both allows you to change the printer and to select the number of copies and so on.

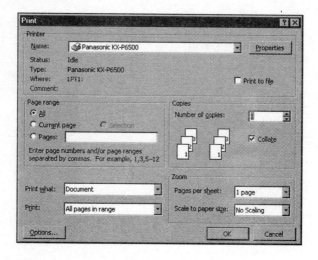

Print your file if you wish.

Close the file.

Numbering paragraphs

Open the file TEST and position the cursor in the first paragraph and then click on the **Numbering** button. The paragraph will be numbered and indented automatically.

Highlight the other paragraphs and click on the **Numbering** button, the numbers should be sequential.

Preview the file and then save it as TESTNUM (remember to pull down the **File** menu and choose **Save As**).

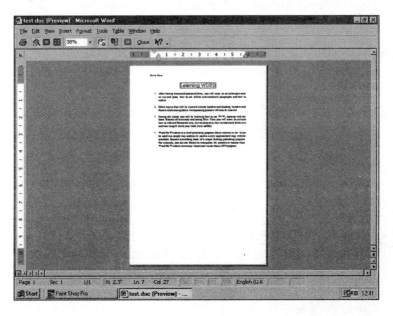

If the numbering does not start with the correct figure, then (after highlighting all the paragraphs) pull down the **Format** menu and select **Bullets** and **Numbering**.

Within this dialog box, choose **Customize** and there is an option called **Start at**. You can change the number to any number you wish.

Bullets

A similar technique to numbering, bullets put a symbol instead of a number at the start of the paragraph (which is indented in the same way as the numbered paragraphs).

Highlight all the numbered paragraphs and click on the **Bullet** button.

Pull down the **Format** menu, and select **Bullets and Numbering.**

Choose another of the bullets and then click on OK. You should now have bulleted paragraphs in place of the numbered ones.

Preview and then save the file (**File** and **Save As**) as TESTBULL.

By using the **Format** and **Bullets** followed by **Customize** and then **Bullet** you can alter the bullets, some of the most original bullets are found in the **Wingdings**® font set.

Close the file.

Search and replace

It is sometimes necessary to search for a specific word and to replace it with another word. This is a technique common to all word processing programs.

Open the file TEST and move the cursor to the top of the file (a quick way of doing this is to hold the **Ctrl** key and while doing so to press the **Home** key). Pull down the **Edit** menu and select **Replace**.

Enter the word to in the **Find what** box and the word three in the **Replace with** box.

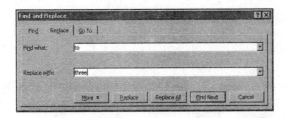

Click on the **Replace All** button and all the occurrences of the word to will be replaced with the word three.

I am sure that since the text is now not making much sense you will want to change it back!

Close the file, without saving the changes.

Inserting clipart

It is easy to add graphics to your work.

Open the file TEST and position the cursor between the second and third paragraphs.

Pull down the **Insert** menu and select **Picture** then **Clip Art**. You will see the **Microsoft Clip Gallery**. Choose **Pictures** (if necessary).

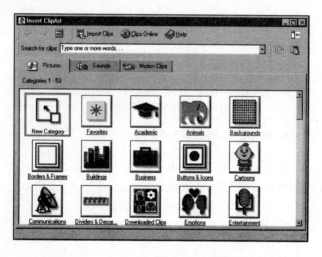

Within this, there are many pictures, select a category and then a picture. Insert your chosen picture into the document and select (by clicking it).

Pull down the **Format** menu (or right-click the image) and select **Picture** and then **Size**. Alter the **Height** to 1" and then click in the **Width** box to (automatically) adjust the width.

Now select **Layout**.

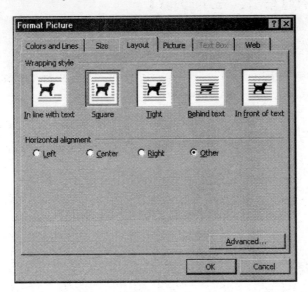

Choose **Square (Wrapping style)** and then **OK**.

Drag the picture to the middle of the page and you will see the text wrap around the picture.

Preview the file.

It should look similar to this.

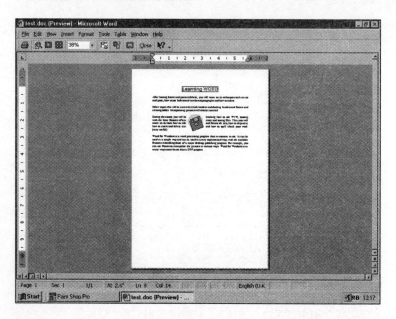

Save the file as TESTFR (**File** and **Save As**) and close it.

> Please note that it is not good practice to use a graphic to split a single text column into two. It makes reading difficult; the exercise is purely to practise the technique of wrapping, not to suggest that this is good layout.

Word Art

Another feature of W4W is **Word Art**. This can be used for logos or any other situation where you want to use fancy lettering.

Open the file TEST and position the cursor just below the title, pull down the **Insert** menu and select **Object**.

From the list, choose **Microsoft Word Art 3**. You will see the **Word Art** module appear.

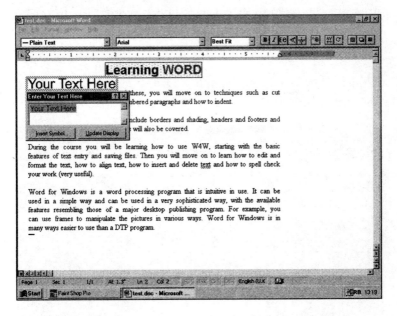

Enter the following (returning at the end of each line).

Your Name

Telephone number

Choose a suitable shape, font, colour, fill, effect, etc., from the selections shown along the toolbar (see below) and click outside the dialog box when finished. To alter the object, simply double-click it.

Once the **Word Art** object is embedded into your document, you can size it to taste and position it.

Select the Word Art object by clicking on it. Pull down the **Format** menu, and **Object** and then **Layout**; finally select **Square** (**Wrapping style**). Alternatively, right-click the object.

Adjust the measurements **Distance From Text (Advanced)** until it looks similar to that shown below.

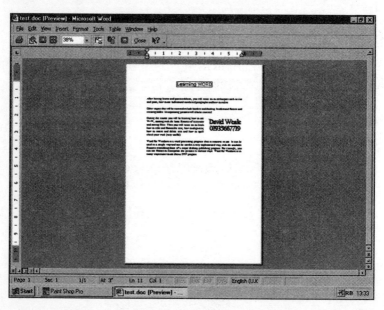

38

Using the Drawing Tools

If you pull down the **View** menu and select **Toolbars**, followed by **Drawing**, you will see the following toolbar (usually along the bottom of the screen).

This contains various shapes, buttons allowing you to alter the colours, insert WordArt, arrows, etc.

Some of these features, e.g. WordArt, offer a different way of using the feature and all are worth looking at and experimenting with.

Save the file as TESTWA and close it.

Counting the number of words

There is often a requirement to know how many words have been used in a document. This is easy in W4W.

Open the file TEST. Pull down the **Tools** menu and select **Word Count** and there it is!

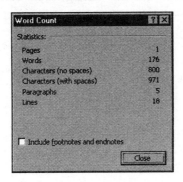

Page Setup

You may want to customise the paper size or the margins for specific pieces of work. The various options (all of which use the **File** and then **Page Setup** commands) include:

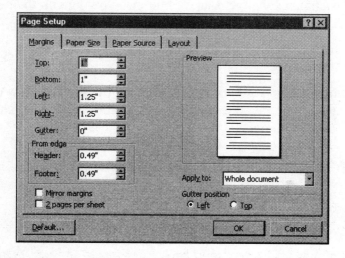

Margins, you can alter the margins for all the text (be careful to distinguish between this technique and indenting which can be applied to individual paragraphs).

Paper Size, here you can change between **Portrait** and **Landscape** orientation and alter the paper size (printers normally use A4).

To practise this, change the orientation of the file to **Landscape** and **preview** it.

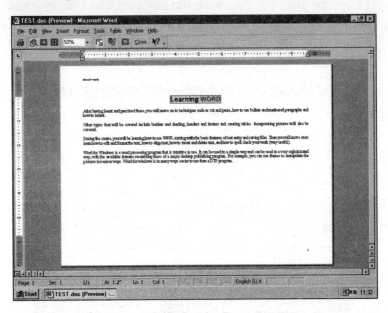

Now alter the orientation back to **Portrait** and **preview** it to see the difference.

Close the file (without saving the changes).

Adding Footnotes

It is often useful to add footnotes to your work to explain words within the text.

Open TESTBULL.

Place the cursor after the phrase W4W (third paragraph) and pull down the **Insert** menu, select **Footnote** and **OK**.

The footnote screen will be displayed.

Type in a footnote (Word for Windows).

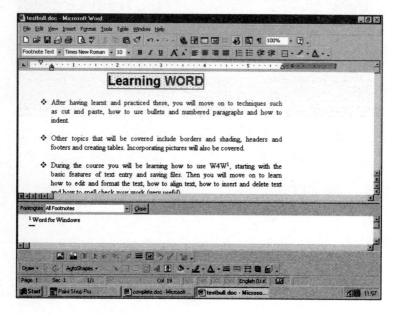

Close the footnote section and then preview the file to see how it looks.

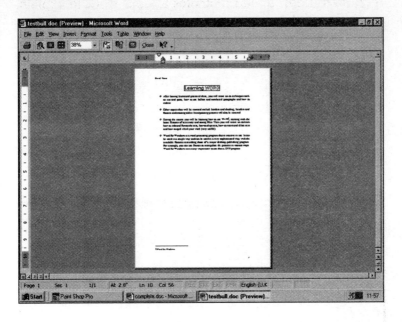

Changing Case

There is a very quick and easy method of changing the case of any character.

Highlight the title, then hold down the **Shift** key, and press the **F3** function key. Repeat this until you have the combination of upper and lower case characters you want.

If you pull down the **Format** menu, followed by **Change Case** you will see a dialog box that gives you more control if you want to alter the case of text.

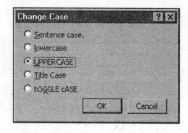

Save the file as TESTBULL and close it.

Creating columns

Open the file TEST; highlight all the text (only – excluding the title), and copy it below itself (twice) using the **Copy** button and then the **Paste** button (so there is three times as much text as originally).

Pull down the **View** menu and select **Print Layout**.

Click on the **Columns** button in the toolbar and highlight two columns.

Your document will now be in two columns, which you can see by previewing the file.

After previewing the text, you may see that the title is slightly strange and is not centred. If this is the case, position the cursor just below the title, pull down the **Insert** menu, and then **Break**, finally selecting **Continuous Section Break**. Position the cursor in the title section and using the **Column** button select single columns and then centre the title.

Insert a **Column break (Insert Break)** before the last paragraph in the initial column (use the **return** key to line up the columns if necessary).

Finally, put a page break just before the last paragraph in the second column.

Preview the file and then save it (**File** and **Save As**) as COLTEST and close it.

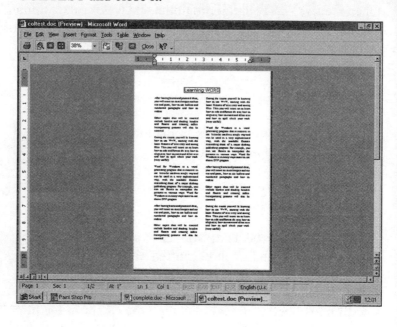

Tables

Most word processing programs have a feature called **Tables**. This helps in laying out columns of words or figures symmetrically.

Create a new file using the **New File** button or by pulling down the **File** menu and selecting **New**.

Click on the **Insert Table** button and highlight a grid of four rows (down) by three columns (across). Enter the following data into the table (using the **tab** key to move between cells).

Week	Activity	Topic
1	Lecture	The Purposes of Accounting
2	Lecture/Practice	Cash Flow Statements
3 - 5	Lecture/Practice	Double Entry Book-keeping

Highlight the table. Click on the **Format** menu and then on **Borders and Shading**. Choose the line style and then click on the **Grid** symbol. At this stage, it is best to be in **Print Layout View** (**View** menu).

Highlight the top row and format the text to bold.

Alter the column widths of the table as necessary by positioning the mouse pointer on the line dividing two columns and then clicking and dragging the line.

Pull down the **Table** menu, select **Table Properties,** and then **Table** and **Center (Alignment)**.

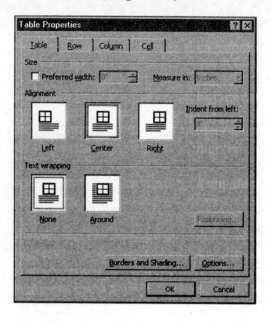

You should now have a table with the grid lines showing when you preview the file. Save the file as TEST1.

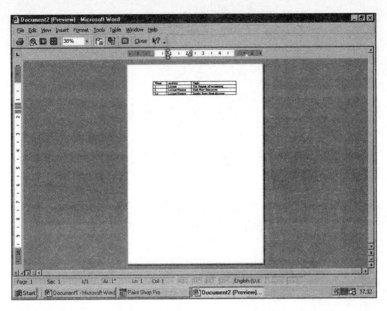

Position the cursor in the very last cell of the table and use the **tab** key to add another row to the table.

Add the following text and preview and save the file

6 - 7	Lecture/Practice	Profit & Loss Accounts

Now add the following column to the table. To do this, position the cursor just beyond the last column and then pull down the **Table** menu and **Select Column** followed by **Insert Columns to the Right**.

Chapter
1-2
Handout
3
4

Centre align the contents of the fourth column and alter the column widths as appropriate.

Highlight the top row of the table and add a shaded pattern to it and a thicker border.

Change the **Page Setup** to **Landscape**, preview, and save the file as TEST1.

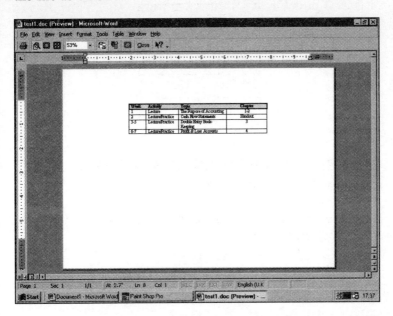

To lay out your table without the borders showing simply select the table and pull down the **Format** menu, select **Borders and Shading** and click the **None** (setting) button.

Close the file.

Using Tab settings

It is also possible to set out your work using **Tabs**; this is messier than using tables.

Open a new file and pull down the **Format** menu, selecting **Tabs**.

Set the tab settings (left, at 1" and 3") by typing in the figure and then clicking the **Set** button.

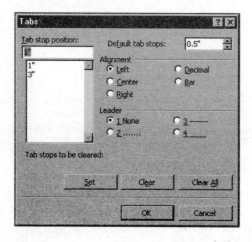

Enter the following text, using the **tab** key to move to the next column and the **return** key at the end of each line.

Week	Activity	Topic
1	Lecture	The Purposes of Accounting
2	Lecture/Practice	Cash Flow Statements
3 - 5	Lecture/Practice	Double Entry Book-keeping

The result should look like this.

Save the file as TABS and close it.

Importing text

You may need to import text from another file.

Open the file TEST and position the cursor at the end of the document (**return**ing to create space as necessary).

Pull down the **Insert** menu and select **File**, select the file TESTBULL and **Insert** it.

Preview the result and then close the file **without** saving the changes.

Text Styles

In order to achieve consistency and to enable you to automatically produce a TOC (table of contents) you can use the **Styles** feature.

Open the file TEST. Add headings to each of the paragraphs, giving them the name Paragraph One, Paragraph Two and so on.

Now click on the first paragraph heading and then on the **Style** button on the toolbar (to the left of the font button), click on the arrow to the right.

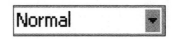

This pulls down a list.

Heading 1

Heading 2

Heading 3

Heading 4

Normal

entry

Comment Text

Default Paragraph Font

Footer

Header

Normal Indent

Page Number

Select **Heading 3** style for the first paragraph heading and then **Heading 4** for the second, **Heading 3** for the third, and **Heading 4** for the fourth.

You can see how it may look in the following illustration.

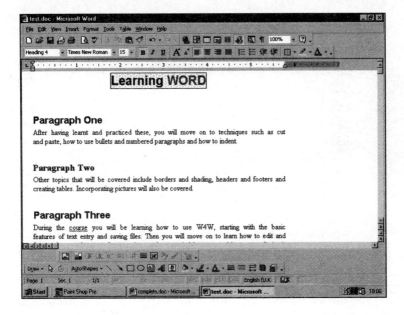

Altering styles

You can alter any style, for example highlight an example of **Heading 3** style.

Pull down the **Format** menu and select **Style**. You will see the following dialog box.

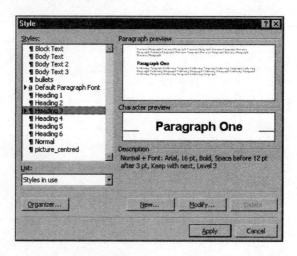

Click on the **Modify** button and then select **Format** and then **Font**. Alter the font type (to **Baskerville Old Face**), the size (to 18 pt) the colour (to **red**) and click on the **OK** button.

On the next screen make sure the **Automatically Update** box is checked and click on **OK** and then on **Apply**.

All the examples of **Heading 3** style will have changed.

To practise, change the style of the other heading's style.

It may look similar to this.

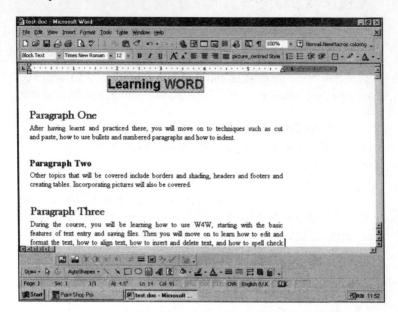

TOC (table of contents)

Insert a **Page Break** before each of the paragraphs (including the first).

Position the cursor at the top of the file (just below the title).

Type in the word `Contents` and format it to Arial 16 point.

Create a table of contents by pulling down the **Insert** menu, followed by **Index and Tables** and finally **Table Of Contents**.

Choose the **Formal** style of TOC (**General Formats**) and ensure that the **Show Levels** is set to **4**.

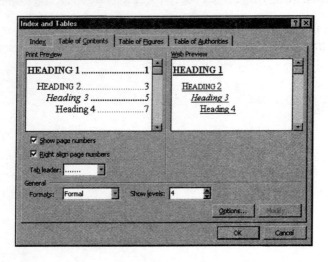

Preview the file.

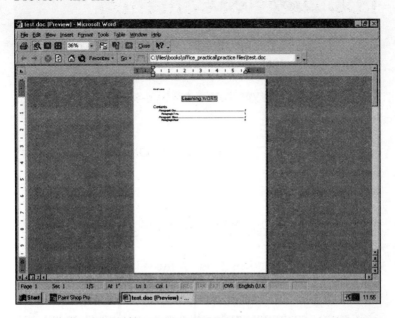

You now have a simple contents page, see how easy it is to produce. If you re-arrange the pages in your document, simply redo the Table of Contents.

Save the file as CONTENTS and close it.

Inserting fields

It is sometimes useful to insert fields into your document (either as body text or as a header/footer).

Examples of fields you may wish to insert are:

Date

Filename

User Information

You can choose from many different fields.

Open a new file and pull down the **View** menu, selecting **Header and Footer**.

Switch to the footer and pull down the **Insert** menu and then **Field**.

From the list of fields, choose **Date and Time**; follow this by clicking the **Options** tab and choosing one of the formats, clicking on the **Add to Field** button.

You should now see the date as your footer, which you can format and align as you wish.

Enter a space after the date and (again) pull down the **Insert** menu and then **Field**, this time select **Document Information** and **FileName**. The filename will be entered as a footer (I find this extremely useful as it enables me to match up files to bits of paper).

Save the file as FIELDS and then press the **F9** function key (after highlighting the footer) to update the field, you should see the footer change to the correct (saved) filename.

Close the file, saving the changes.

Templates

A template contains settings such as fonts, page layout, formatting, and styles.

You can create your own templates to suit your needs; for example, a template could be created for letters. This template may contain your name and address, the date, and you can set the fonts, margins, etc., as you desire.

Create templates to store different layouts, formatting, styles, and so on. Once you have created a template, you can use it without having to recreate the formatting, page layout, margins, text, and so on

To create a template, enter the text you want to appear, e.g. your address, set the margins and so on.

Then save the file, making sure that you save it as a **Document Template (*.dot)** in the **Save as type** box.

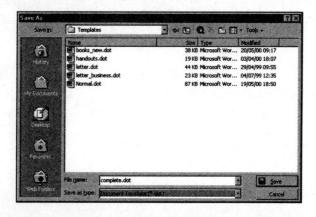

Your new template will appear when you pull down the **File** menu, selecting **New** and **More Word Templates**.

Exercise

Open a new (empty) file and make the following changes.

Enter your address at the top, right-aligned and formatted to whatever font/font size you consider appropriate.

Just below your address, insert a date field.

Press the **return** key a couple of times, enter the word Dear and justify the text.

Alter the margins to 2" (left, right, top, bottom)

Create a footer with the filename (using **Insert** and **Field**), right-aligned in italic and eight-point font size.

Pull down the **File** menu and select **Save As**, make sure that you alter the **Save as type** to **Document Template**, save the file as LETTERTEMP and close the file.

To check this has worked satisfactorily, pull down the **File** menu, select **New** and **More Word Templates** and you should see your new template appear in the list.

Double-click the template and it will appear on screen, you can then add the text and save it as a normal document.

Mailmerging

Mailmerging means to merge a list of names and addresses (data) with a (standard) letter.

Begin by creating a new file, enter your address, and insert the date. Right-align all this text.

Pull down the **Tools** menu and select **Mail Merge** and then **Options**.

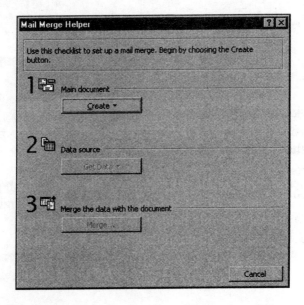

Click the **Create** button and select **Form Letters**.

Then click the **Get Data** button followed by **Create Data Source**.

You will see the following dialog box.

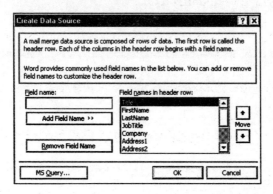

Click on **Remove Field Name** (after selecting the **Field Name**) until only following fields are left.

First Name

Last Name

Company

Address 1

Address 2

City

State

Postal Code

Finally, click on the **OK** button. You will be prompted to save the file, call it MERGE.

Next click on the **Edit Data Source** and enter the following data into the **Data Form** that appears. Use the **tab** key to move onto the next line.

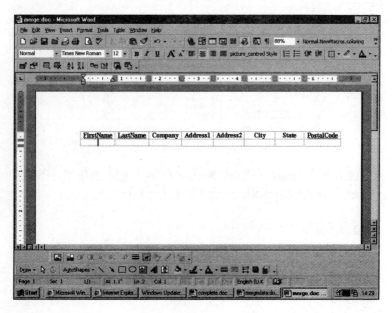

joe

smith

smith hydraulic pumps plc

the old smithy

new town industrial park

somerton

somerset

ta21 6tr

Use the **tab** key to move onto the next line and enter the next details.

sally

jukins

happy holidays

34 high street

(blank line)

oldtown

dorset

bh3 6tr

Highlight the table and pull down the **Format** menu, selecting **Change Case** and select **Title Case**.

Save the file and close it.

Then enter the fields into the letter by clicking on the **Insert Merge Field** button, **return**ing to create a new line.

Insert Merge Field ▾

Make sure the fields are left-aligned and you should see a letter similar to this.

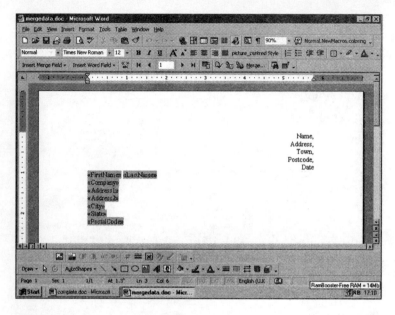

Save the file as MERGEDATA.

To merge the data with the letter, click on the
Merge to New Document button on the toolbar.

The data should be merged to a new document (below) with a separate page for each address.

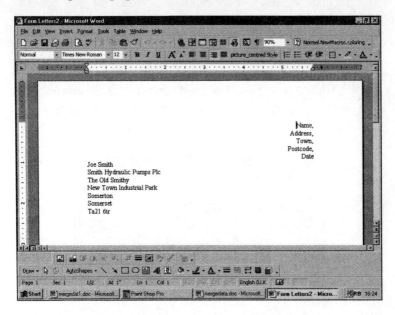

Preview the file and you should see each address appear in sequence.

Save the file as LETTERS and close all the files.

Customising the toolbars

The toolbar buttons and layout are aimed at the general user and you may have requirements that are more specific, for example, you may want to remove some of the existing buttons and add others.

To do this, you need to pull down the **Tools** menu, followed by **Customize**. Select the **Commands** tab and you should see the following dialog box.

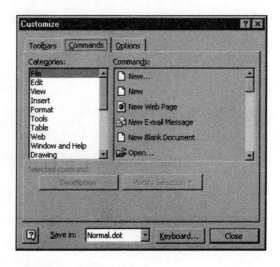

To add new buttons, find the button you want (first select **Categories** and then **Commands**) and drag it onto the toolbar in the position you want it to appear.

To remove buttons, simply drag the buttons off the toolbar (the dialog box – above – must be open).

You can do this with any toolbar you have visible on the screen (remember that to make a toolbar appear on screen, pull down the **View** menu followed by **Toolbars** and click the one you want).

To practise, remove the buttons for **Document Map** and **Web Toolbar** and insert the following new buttons (**Format** category).

This feature is available within any of the Office programs.

Excel

Starting off

The Excel screen (shown opposite) is divided into rows (across) and columns (down). Rows are numbered and columns are lettered. The screen is divided by gridlines into cells, each cell having a unique address, e.g. A1 or C9.

The following can be entered into cells.

- Text (words)

- Numbers

- Formulae (calculations)

- Graphics

- Objects (Word Art, Equations, etc.)

Moving around the worksheet

You can move around by using the cursor keys or by clicking the mouse in a cell.

Entering text or numbers

Move to the cell into which you want to enter text or numbers and type the text or number.

Then either hit the **return** key or use the **cursor keys** to move the cursor to the next cell.

Enter the data (shown below) into the worksheet.

	A	B	C	D
1		january		
2	sally	100	200	150
3	bob	90	75	125
4	julian	110	80	90

Saving your work

It is vital to save your work regularly (computers can malfunction).

Click on the **Save** button on the toolbar and save the file (call it PRAC1) to the folder you want to (it is much better to save to a hard disc rather than a floppy disc as the process is faster and more reliable).

The **Save (As)** screen is shown for reference.

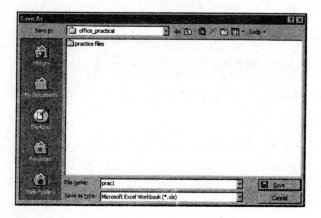

So far you have entered text, numbers and saved the file.

Copying cells

One of the advantages of a spreadsheet (over paper) is that you can copy data and formulae quickly and easily.

Click the mouse in cell **B1** and move the mouse pointer to the bottom right corner of the cell until it becomes a thin cross shape (called a fill handle).

Now click and drag the cross shape to cell **D1** and then let go of the mouse button. You will see that the program has inserted the correct months into the cells.

Aligning cells

To alter the formatting of cells, you need to highlight the cells.

To highlight, click the mouse in the initial cell and drag the (large cross) so that all the cells you want to format are highlighted (the initial cell will be included but not highlighted).

Highlight cells **B1** to **D1**.

Click the **Align Right** button on the toolbar.

The headings will now line up with the numbers - numbers should always be right-aligned so the hundreds, tens and units are underneath each other - remember your schooldays.

Now add the words (shown below) in the appropriate cells.

A5   total

E1   total

Right-align cell **E1**.

Your worksheet should now look like this.

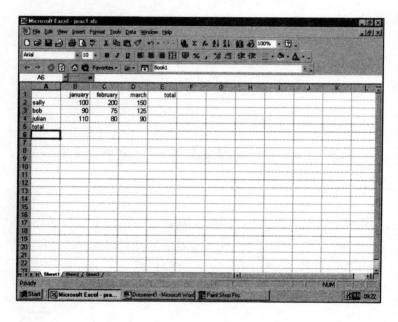

Entering formulae

It is important to understand the need to enter a calculation (rather than the answer) into the appropriate cells. If you enter a formula and then alter any of the original data, the calculation will show the change.

Click the mouse in cell **B5** and then click on the **AutoSum** button on the toolbar.

You should see the following formula entered in the cell.

	A	B	C	D	E
1		january	february	march	total
2	sally	100	200	150	
3	bob	90	75	125	
4	julian	110	80	90	
5	total	=SUM(B2:B4)			

Hit the **return** key and the answer will appear.

Now copy the formula in cell **B5** across to cells **C5** to **D5** (in the same way you copied the months earlier).

Click in cell **E2** and use the **AutoSum** button to calculate the total for Sally.

Now copy the formula in **E2** to cells **E3** to **E5**.

Save your file (as PRAC1) using the **Save** button.

It should look like this.

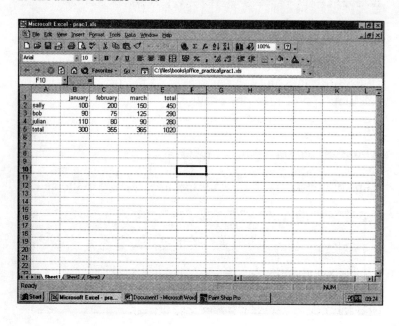

Inserting rows and columns

To insert a blank row or column click the cursor in the cell **after** the position you want to insert a row or column and then pull down the **Insert** menu and select **Rows** or **Columns**.

Click the cursor in cell **A1** and insert a row.

Enter the following text in cell **A1**.

Direct Sales Co.

Centring text (across columns)

Highlight the cells **A1** to **E1**. Then click on the **Merge and Center** button on the toolbar. The title should now be centred across the columns.

Altering the fonts

Click in cell **A1** and using the **Font Size** button, alter the font size to 14 (point).

Then use the **Font** button to alter the font to **Times New Roman**.

Finally, use the **Font Color** button to alter the colour to **Red** (click on the arrow to the right to display the colours).

To practise, alter the fonts of the months and the people's names to whatever font, size, and colour you choose (try to be sensible).

If you pull down the **Format** menu, select **Cells** and then **Font**, you have even more variety.

Borders and patterns

To make data stand out, you can alter the font, size, and colour. Another method is to use borders and patterns.

To try this, highlight cells **A6** to **E6**, then pull down the **Format** menu, and select **Cells** followed by **Border**.

You should see the following dialog box.

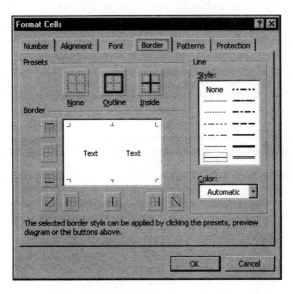

Choose the **(Line) Style**, **Color** and then click on the **Outline** button (you must click the **Outline** button last). Finally, click on **OK**.

Your cells should now have a border (you may need to click the mouse away to see the border).

If you wish, you can add shading or patterns by the same method (only choosing **Patterns** rather than **Border**).

Place a border around the months and **Save** the results. The worksheet may look similar to this.

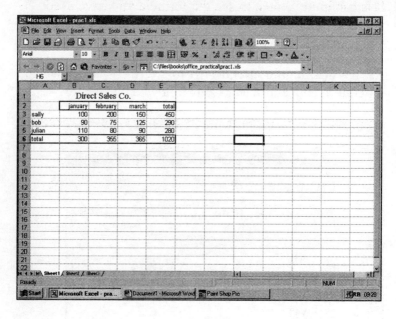

Viewing the formula

It is useful to be able to see the formula you have used. To do this hold down the **Ctrl** key and then press the key above the **tab** key (to the left of the **1** key).

This should display the formula (repeat this to return to the figures).

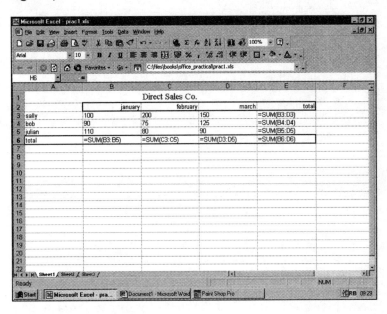

Page Setup

At this stage (before printing the worksheet), it is worthwhile exploring the various layout options.

Pull down the **File** menu and then select **Page Setup**. You will see the following screen.

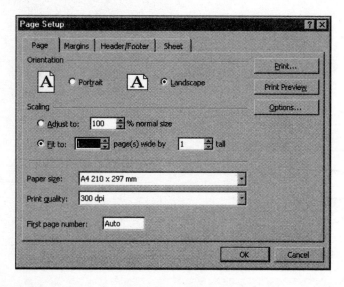

You may want to select **Landscape** and **Fit to** (one page) from this screen (to select the items, ensure a dot is shown by each - as you can see in the example).

Next select **Margins** and tick the **Center on page** boxes at the bottom (as shown in the example below).

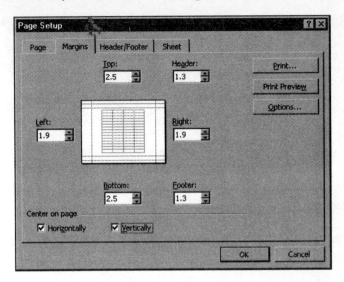

Finally select **Header/Footer** and you will be able to add your own headers and footers to the worksheet. Click on **Custom Header** and enter the data described on the next page.

To insert the date or filename use the appropriate button.

Date

Filename

The example shows three headers, my name, the filename, and the date. Footers work in a similar way.

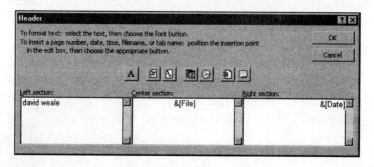

Using headers and footers is important as they allow you to identify the printout far more easily.

Add your name, the filename, and the date as a header, return to the worksheet.

Previewing the worksheet

To save paper and time it is best to preview the worksheet before printing it.

Click on the **Preview** button and you should see the following screen.

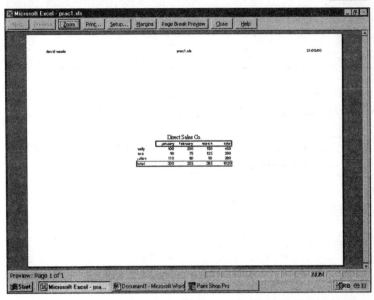

Click on the **Close** button to return to the worksheet.

Printing your worksheet

To print the worksheet, click on the **Print** button on the toolbar (if you want to have more choices, pull down the **File** menu and select **Print**).

To practise, print the worksheet and then the formulae (separately).

Closing the file

Save the file, then pull down the **File** menu, and select **Close**.

Starting a new file

Click on the **New** button on the toolbar and a new worksheet will appear.

A new exercise

Please enter the new worksheet, do not worry if the data does not fit into the cells, this will be dealt with in the next section.

	A	B	C	D
1	SALES FIGURES			
2	Salesperson	Year ended	Year ended	Difference
3		31-Dec-99	31-Dec-98	
4	Smith.C	24000	26000	
5	Jules.B	46000	45000	
6	Norris.T	85000	82000	
7	Torr.M	66000	99000	
8	Bates.N	35000	32000	

Altering column (or row) width

If you enter too much text to fit in the cell, or if you alter the font size, then all the data may not fit into the cell.

With numbers, you may see the following symbol. This symbol shows that the column is not wide enough to display the numbers correctly.

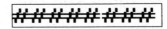

To alter the width manually, move the mouse pointer to the divide between two column letters when it will become a two-arrowhead cross.

Click and drag the divider until you are happy.

You can also alter the width by highlighting the column(s) and pulling down the **Format** menu and selecting **Column** and then **Width**.

Save the file as PRAC2.

Entering formulae

You have already used the **AutoSum** button, however you may want to enter other formulae.

In this case you are going to calculate the difference in sales between the years (the figures represent pounds).

To enter the formula carry out the following steps.

Click in cell **D4** and then enter an = (equals) sign (all formulae begin with this sign - the **AutoSum** formula adds it automatically).

Click the mouse in cell **B4**.

Enter a - (minus) sign.

Click the mouse pointer in cell **C4**.

Hit the **return** key.

If you have carried this out correctly then the answer should appear in cell **D4**.

If you click back on cell **D4,** you should see the formula in the **Formula Bar**.

Copy the formula from **D4** to **D8**.

Total the first column (using the **AutoSum** button).

Copy the total across the columns.

Add another person (after **Bates**). The name is **Harris.R** and the figures are 20800 and 19900 respectively. Calculate the difference by copying the formula from the cell above (if the program does not do this automatically).

The totals have not changed. You will need to redo the formula for the totals (if you insert a new row other than at the top or bottom of the table then the formula will automatically be recalculated).

Sorting the data

Highlight the data including the names (but **only** rows **4** to **9**, you do not want to sort the headings or the totals).

Pull down the **Data** menu and select **Sort**. You will see the following dialog box.

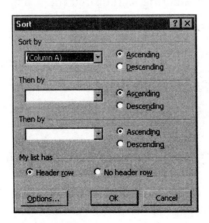

Make sure that it looks like this (**Sort by** is **Column A**) and then click on the **OK** button.

The data should be sorted and look like this.

	A	B	C	D
1	SALES FIGURES			
2	Salesperson	Year ended	Year ended	Difference
3		31-Dec-99	31-Dec-98	
4	Bates.N	35000	32000	3000
5	Harris.R	20800	19900	900
6	Jules.B	46000	45000	1000
7	Norris.T	85000	82000	3000
8	Smith.C	24000	26000	-2000
9	Torr.M	66000	99000	-33000
10		276800	303900	-27100

Now format the worksheet in the following ways.

- ❏ Centre the title across the columns.

- ❏ Alter the fonts (size, type and colour) and add borders/shading as required (be sensible!).

- ❏ Align column headings (the columns with numbers) to the right.

- ❏ Landscape orientation.

- ❏ Fit to one page.

- ❏ Centre horizontally and vertically on the page.

- ❏ Insert a header (your name) and footers (date and filename).

Preview both the figures **and** the formulae (and print if you wish to).

The result may look like this (figures first, then formulae).

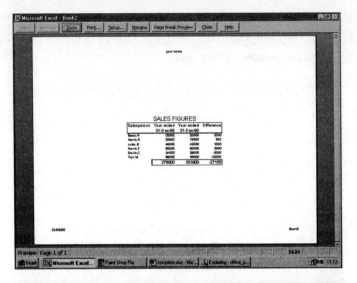

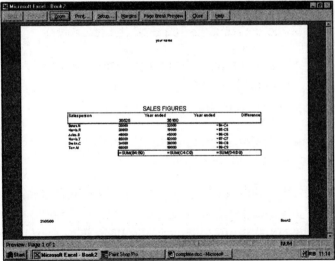

Save the file as PRAC2.

AutoFormat

A quick way of formatting a worksheet is to **highlight** all the data you want to format, then pull down the **Format** menu and select **AutoFormat**.

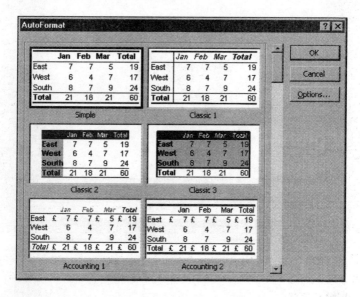

You can choose from a variety of different formats, which once applied to your worksheet can be altered.

Note the **Options** button, this enables you to make decisions about the formatting.

Normally, if you want to apply the **AutoFormat** then do so **before** any other formatting since the **AutoFormat** will overwrite some of the changes you make before you apply it.

Apply one of the **AutoFormats** to your file.

It may look similar to this when previewed.

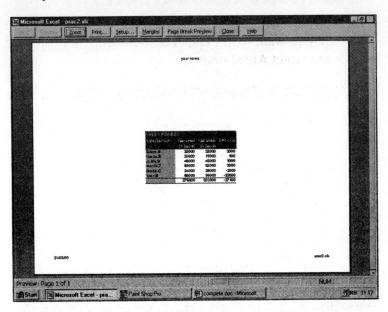

Pull down the **File** menu and select **Save As** so you can alter the file name, save your revised version as PRAC3 and close it.

Another new exercise

Enter a new worksheet (adjusting the column widths as necessary).

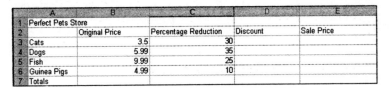

	A	B	C	D	E
1	Perfect Pets Store				
2		Original Price	Percentage Reduction	Discount	Sale Price
3	Cats	3.5	30		
4	Dogs	5.99	35		
5	Fish	9.99	25		
6	Guinea Pigs	4.99	10		
7	Totals				

Arithmetic calculations

The symbols used for arithmetic operators are as follows:

Addition	+
Subtraction	-
Multiplication	*
Division	/

Remember that **all** formulae have to begin with the = sign.

Now calculate the **Discount** Column by working out the percentages (**Original Price** times **Percentage Reduction**) - use the % key for the percentage. You can see the formula in the illustration.

	A	B	C	D	E
1	Perfect Pets Store				
2		Original Price	Percentage Reduction	Discount	Sale Price
3	Cats	3.5	30	=B3*C3%	
4	Dogs	5.99	35		
5	Fish	9.99	25		
6	Guinea Pigs	4.99	10		
7	Totals				

Calculate the **Sale Price** column (**Original Price** minus **Discount**).

Copy these down to the other rows and total the columns.

At this stage, your worksheet should correspond closely to this.

	A	B	C	D	E
1	Perfect Pets Store				
2		Original Price	Percentage Reduction	Discount	Sale Price
3	Cats	3.5	30	1.05	2.45
4	Dogs	5.99	35	2.0965	3.8935
5	Fish	9.99	25	2.4975	7.4925
6	Guinea Pigs	4.99	10	0.499	4.491
7	Totals	24.47	100	6.143	18.327

Formatting numbered cells

As you can see, the number of decimal places varies from cell to cell. This is poor layout and makes the figures difficult to read. You should be consistent with the number of decimal places within a column.

Highlight all the numbered cells and pull down the **Format** menu, choose **Cells**, and then **Number**. From the list select **Currency** and then **2** decimal places (this should be the default).

All your numbers should now have pound signs in front and have two decimal places.

Obviously, this is incorrect for the **Percentage Reduction** column, so format this to **Number** (zero decimal places).

Cell alignment

You can make the layout more attractive by altering the alignment of cells. In this example, the column headings are too wide.

Highlight cells **B2** to **E2** and **Format**, **Column** and **Width** (to 10). With the cells **B2** to **E2** still highlighted, **Format**, **Row,** and **Height** (to 25).

With cells **B2** to **E2** still highlighted, pull down the **Format** menu, and select **Cells** and then **Alignment**.

Alter the settings to those shown below, the text will wrap around and the worksheet will look more sensibly laid out.

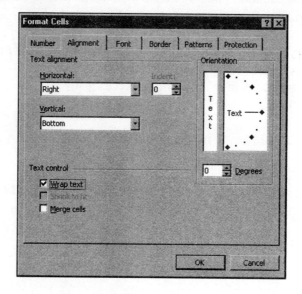

Use the following formatting.

- ❏ Landscape orientation.

- ❏ Fit to one page.

- ❏ Centre horizontally and vertically on the page.

- ❏ Header (your name) and footers (date and filename).

- ❏ Centre the business name across the columns.

- ❏ Alter the fonts (size, type and colour) and add borders/shading as required (be sensible!).

Save the file as PRAC4.

Preview both the figures **and** the formulae (and print if you wish to).

The result (when previewed) could look similar to this.

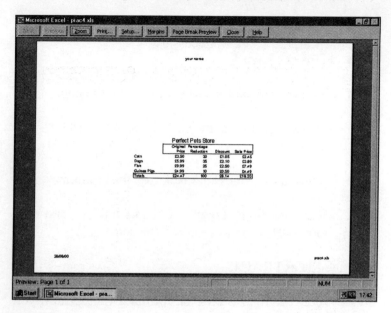

Close the file.

The next exercise

Enter the data shown below into a new worksheet, adjusting column width as necessary.

	A	B	C	D
1	Personal Expenditure Analysis (£)			
2	Item	Jan		
3	Mortgage	50.5	52	41.2
4	Electricity	3.5	5.2	12.67
5	Rates	7.6	7.6	7.6
6	Food	41.26	45.4	39.3
7	Motor	9.9	10.89	10.5
8	Holidays	3.5	3.5	3.5
9	Insurance	3.9	3.9	3.9
10	Fun	11.1	12.21	11.45
11	Savings	20	20	20
12	Total Expenses			
13	Income	155	155	155
14	Excess			

Copy the month across to the other columns.

Total the expenditure for Jan and copy this across.

Calculate the **Excess** for each month (**Income** minus **Total Expenses**).

Save the file as PRAC5.

Functions

You have already used the **SUM** function, here are some more functions, which you can enter manually.

Add these column headings to your worksheet (columns **E** to **H**).

	A	B	C	D	E	F	G	H
1	Personal Expenditure Analysis (£)							
2	Item	Jan	Feb	Mar	Total	Minimum	Maximum	Average

Use the **AutoSum** to calculate the first total (cell **E3**).

In the **Minimum** column, (cell **F3**) enter the following formula (do not type in the cell references, but click the mouse in the first cell and drag to include all the cells you want - this works the same as typing in the cell references but is more accurate and quicker).

=MIN(B3:D3)

Do the same for **G3** and **H3**, substituting **MAX** and **AVERAGE** respectively in place of the word **MIN**.

Highlight cells **E3** to **H3** and copy them down (together).

Now format the worksheet to:

- [ ] Format the figures to two decimal places (but no pound sign) - use **Format**, **Cells**, **Number**, and **Number** (again).

- [ ] Alter the fonts (size, type and colour) and add borders/shading as required - you may want to use **AutoFormat**.

- [ ] Centre the title across the columns.

- [ ] Align column headings (the columns with numbers) to the right and alter the column widths as desired.

- [ ] Landscape orientation.

- [ ] Fit to one page.

- [ ] Centre horizontally and vertically on the page.

- [ ] Include a header (your name) and footers (date and filename).

Preview both the figures and the formulae (and print if you wish to). It could look similar to this when previewed.

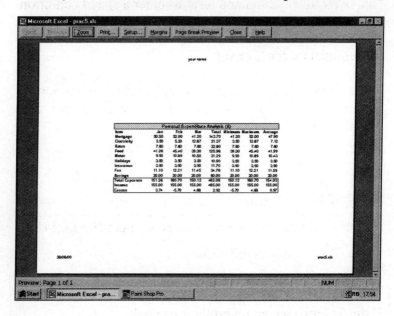

Save and close the file.

Conditional Function

This is the **IF** function and tests whether a stated condition is true or false. The structure is:

=IF(condition, true, false)

The condition is tested and if true then the true section of the function is carried out, if the condition is not true then the false section is carried out.

Example

=IF(it's raining, carry an umbrella, leave the umbrella at home)

the condition is **IF it's raining**

if this is **true** then an umbrella is carried

if the condition is **false** (it is not raining) then leave the umbrella at home

Symbols used in this function

Greater than	>
Less than	<
Greater than or equal to	>=
Less than or equal to	<=

Applying this to a spreadsheet

Create the following worksheet, save it as PRAC6.

	A	B	C	D	E	F
1			the mobile phone company			
2		jan	feb	mar	total	bonus
3	sally	100	150	180	430	
4	fred	190	120	200	510	
5	julie	110	110	125	345	
6	total	400	380	505	1285	

You are told that a bonus is paid to the staff. If the total sales for the three months exceed £500 then a bonus of 10% of the total sales is payable, otherwise there is no bonus.

With the cursor in cell F3, enter the following formulae.

=IF(E3>500,E3*10%,0)

Thus the condition tests if the total sales are greater then £500, if this is true then the bonus is 10% of the sales, if the condition is false then no bonus is paid.

Copy it down to **F5**.

You should see the following result.

	A	B	C	D	E	F
1			the mobile phone company			
2		jan	feb	mar	total	bonus
3	sally	100	150	180	430	0
4	fred	190	120	200	510	51
5	julie	110	110	125	345	0
6	total	400	380	505	1285	

Exercise

Enter the following data into a worksheet and enter a function to work out the bonus on the following basis.

If the total sales are less than £1000, a bonus of 5% of total sales is paid, otherwise a bonus of 10% is paid.

Format the worksheet to your own satisfaction.

	A	B	C	D	E
1		philip	janet	cyril	samantha
2	july	250	350	660	550
3	august	470	550	210	440
4	september	660	870	120	310
5	total				
6	bonus				

Your results should be the same as shown below.

	A	B	C	D	E
1		philip	janet	cyril	samantha
2	july	250	350	660	550
3	august	470	550	210	440
4	september	660	870	120	310
5	total	1380	1770	990	1300
6	bonus	138	177	49.5	130

The formulae for the first two people are shown below.

	A	B	C
1		philip	janet
2	july	250	350
3	august	470	550
4	september	660	870
5	total	=SUM(B2:B4)	=SUM(C2:C4)
6	bonus	=IF(B5<1000,B5*5%,B5*10%)	=IF(C5<1000,C5*5%,C5*10%)

Pivot Tables

Pivot tables are a method of arranging and summarising data. A table is used to summarize data and you can show different summaries of the data.

Enter the following data into a worksheet.

order amount	order date	product	name
20	12-Dec	dog food	pets & ponds
33	16-Nov	sand	perfect pets
12	15-Nov	sand	pets & ponds
65	21-Nov	dog food	dogs forever
11	17-Dec	sand	fun fishes
41	11-Nov	dog food	perfect pets
36	18-Dec	dog food	dogs forever
56	19-Nov	feed	fun fishes
33	11-Nov	dog food	fun fishes

Highlight the data and pull down the **Data** menu, selecting **Pivot Table and PivotChart Report**.

You will see the following dialog box, accept the default settings, and move onto the next.

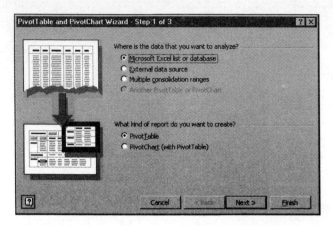

Again, if you highlighted the data correctly, this should be shown below.

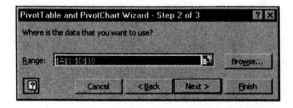

Next choose where you want to place the new pivot table, the default is fine, but you need to select the data you want to appear in the table, so before moving on, click the **Layout** button.

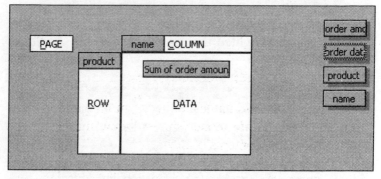

Drag the field names onto the table grid as shown above, click **OK** and then **Finish**.

You will see the pivot table shown.

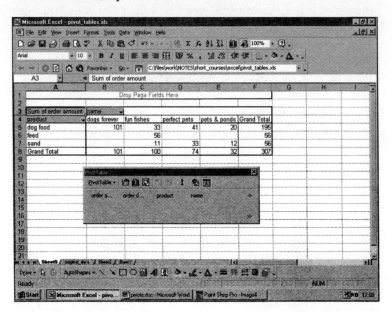

By dragging the field names, either from the table itself or from the **Pivot Table** menu (shown below the table) you can rearrange the contents of the table.

For example, drag the **name** field off the table and then drag the **order date** field onto the table in its place. Your pivot table should now look like this.

Sum of order amount	order date							
product	11-Nov	15-Nov	16-Nov	19-Nov	21-Nov	12-Dec	17-Dec	18-Dec
dog food	74				65	20		36
feed				56				
sand		12	33				11	
Grand Total	74	12	33	56	65	20	11	36

There are many ways to manipulate a pivot table. It is now up to you to experiment.

Save the file as PIVOTS and close it.

Lookup

This function enables you to extract data from a table. When you know the value in one column, you can automatically find the corresponding value in the next column.

For example, if you have a list of descriptions, and prices, you can find the price of an item when you type in the appropriate description.

Add the following data to a new worksheet.

	A	B
1	pet	sale price
2	cat	3.85
3	dog	17.32
4	fish	11.23
5	budgie	14.65
6	mouse	6.99
7	snake	9.65
8		
9	pet	price

For the **Lookup** function to work properly the column you are looking at must be sorted into ascending order so sort column **A**.

Position the cursor in cell **B10**.

Click the **Paste Function** button on the toolbar.
Select the **Lookup & Reference** category and
then **Lookup** from the list on the right.

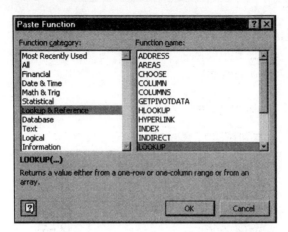

Click **OK** and then accept the next screen.

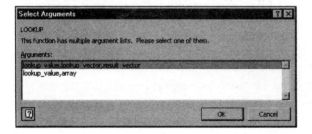

Enter the following data into the next dialog box and click the **OK** button.

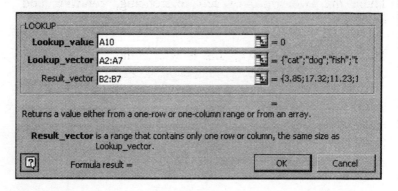

Now enter the name of any of the pets into cell **A10** and you will see the price shown in the adjoining cell.

	A	B
1	pet	sale price
2	cat	3.85
3	dog	17.32
4	fish	11.23
5	budgie	14.65
6	mouse	6.99
7	snake	9.65
8		
9	pet	price
10	dog	17.32

What the function has done is to look up a value in the first column and find the corresponding value in the adjacent column.

Save the file as PRAC6 and close it.

Absolute referencing

There are two types of cell referencing, **relative,** and **absolute**.

The default is **relative**; this is where the cell reference changes as you copy a formulae from one cell to another.

However, it is possible that you may not want this to happen. To fix the cell so that when you copy it, the formulae does not alter, you need to add the **$** sign to the cell reference which creates an absolute reference.

$A4   This makes the column reference absolute so that it will not change, although the row reference will as it is still relative.

A$4   Here the row reference is absolute but not the column reference.

A4   Both the row and column references are absolute.

Enter the following into a worksheet using the **currency** button to add £ signs to the per unit prices.

	A	B	C	D	E	F	G
1	capacious cats						
2		jan	feb	mar	apr	may	jun
3	sales						
4	purchases						
5	profit						
6							
7	unit sold	10	12	15	9	16	20
8	sale price per unit	£ 15.00					
9							
10	units purchased	11	13	16	11	14	17
11	cost price per unit	£ 9.00					

You want to multiply the sale price per unit by the number of units sold in each month. Enter the formulae into **B3** (=B7*B8).

Highlight the reference to B8 in the formulae bar and then use the **F4** function key to toggle the address until it becomes **$B8**.

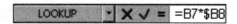

```
LOOKUP    ▾ X ✓ =  =B7*$B8
```

Then copy it across.

Carry out the same process with the purchases and then enter a formula for the profit and copy this across.

Look at the formulae for the worksheet; you can see the difference between the relative and absolute addresses after they have been copied.

	A	B	C	D
1				capacious cats
2		jan	feb	
3	sales	=B7*$B8	=C7*$B8	=D7*$B8
4	purchases	=B10*$B11	=C10*$B11	=D10*$B11
5	profit	=B3-B4	=C3-C4	=D3-D4

The final answer should look similar to this.

		jan	feb	mar	apr	may	jun
1	capacious cats						
2		jan	feb	mar	apr	may	jun
3	sales	£ 150.00	£ 180.00	£ 225.00	£ 135.00	£ 240.00	£ 300.00
4	purchases	£ 99.00	£ 117.00	£ 144.00	£ 99.00	£ 126.00	£ 153.00
5	profit	£ 51.00	£ 63.00	£ 81.00	£ 36.00	£ 114.00	£ 147.00
6							
7	unit sold	10	12	15	9	16	20
8	sale price per unit	£ 15.00					
9							
10	units purchased	11	13	16	11	14	17
11	cost price per unit	£ 9.00					

Save the file as PRAC7.

Freezing panes

If you have a large worksheet, you may want to scroll the data while keeping the headings static.

Using the exercise PRAC7, position the cursor in cell **B3** and then pull down the **Window** menu and select **Freeze Panes**. You will see a vertical and horizontal line appear.

The position of these will be determined by the position of the cursor when you started the process.

This will have the effect of freezing the column **or** row headings but letting you scroll the rest of the data using the vertical and horizontal scroll bars.

To remove the effect, pull down the **Windows** menu and **Unfreeze Panes**.

Charts and Graphs

One of the best ways of communicating numerical data is in the form of a chart. Many people find numbers a little frightening but can assimilate quite complex numerical information if it is visual in nature.

The Chart Wizard

Open the file called PRAC1 and highlight all the data (except the bottom total row) - (i.e. highlight cells **A1** to **E5**).

Click the mouse pointer on the **Chart Wizard** button on the toolbar to begin the process.

You will be presented with a series of dialog boxes into which you enter data or instructions. Enter the data shown in the illustrations below.

The first of these lets you select the chart type you want. In this case, the **Column** is a good choice.

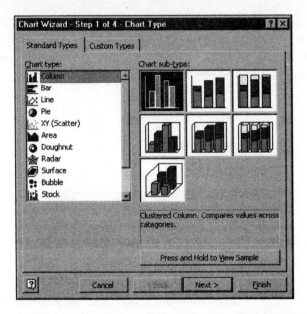

Be careful to choose chart types that show your data to best advantage, i.e. communicate it clearly.

The next screen allows you to alter the way in which the series are shown.

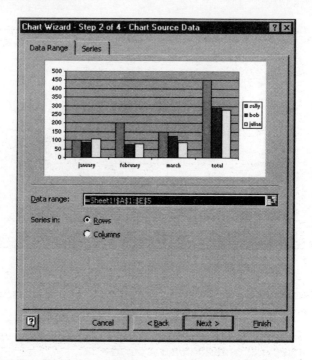

You can select either **Rows** or **Columns**; choose the one that shows the data in the most effective way.

On the next screen, you enter the **Chart title** and the **X** and **Y**-axis labels.

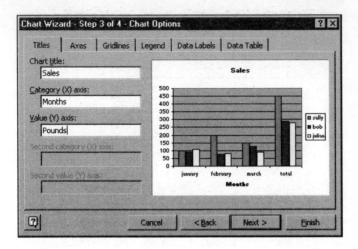

The final screen gives you two choices, I suggest **very strongly** that you select **As new sheet**. This will give you far more control and flexibility over your chart.

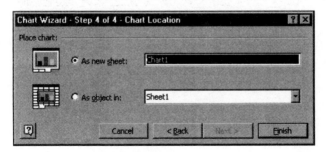

Assuming your have made the same choices, your chart
will look like this.

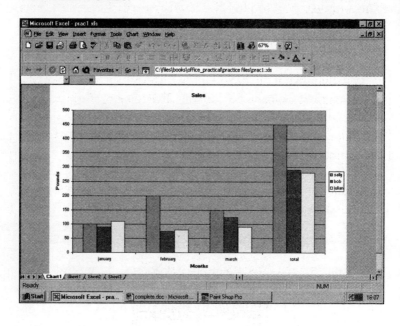

Altering the look of the chart

The simplest way to alter the chart is to click on the **Chart Wizard** and alter the **Chart type**. You can alter the choices you originally made and produce a different chart.

If you ever want to create two different charts from the same data, it is best to use the **Edit** menu followed by **Move or Copy Sheet** to create a copy which contains all the data, formatting, headers and footers and so on and then alter the copy.

The dialog box is shown for reference; note that you should ensure that the **Create a copy** box is ticked.

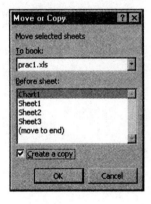

Altering the text font & alignment

You can select any text within the chart by double-clicking it and a dialog box will be displayed allowing you to make changes to the look of the text.

For example, if you double-click the title, you will see the following dialog box, which has three sections

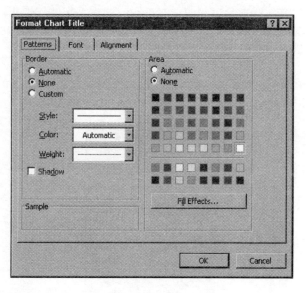

In **Patterns,** you can add a **Border** and/or alter the **Chart Title** area.

Font enables you to change the font type, size, and colour.

In **Alignment** you can alter the **Orientation** (by dragging the **Text** line within this section) and **Text Alignment**.

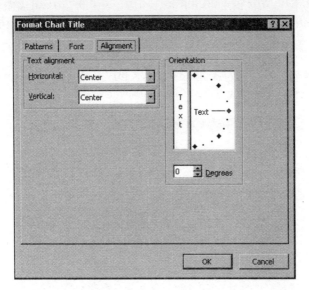

I suggest you experiment with each of these (remember to use the **Undo** button on the toolbar if you make a mess).

Altering the chart

Similarly you can double-click any other part of the chart (e.g. bars, columns) and alter how it looks using the dialog boxes that appear.

For example, if you double-click any of the columns in the chart you will see this dialog box.

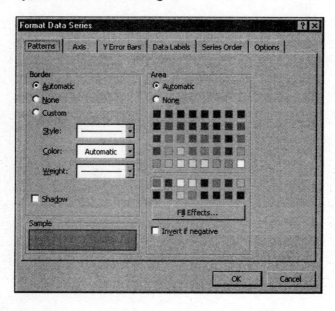

By selecting e.g. **Custom (Border)** or **Fill Effects (Area)**, you can alter the look of the column.

Headers & Footers

These work in exactly the same way as in worksheets (**View** menu). Add your name as a header and the date and filename as footers to your chart.

I have made various changes to the original chart and added headers and footers; see what you can do.

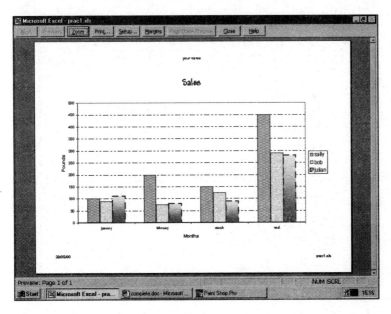

Changing the names of the worksheets

Now you have more than one worksheet in the file, it is useful to make the names of the worksheets meaningful.

Double-click the name (i.e. **Chart 1**) along the bottom of the screen and type in **Direct sales chart**.

Do the same for the chart calling it **Direct sales spreadsheet**.

| ◀ ◀ ▶ ▶ \ **Direct sales chart** ╱ Direct sales spreadsheet ╱ |

Save and close the file.

Adding legends and X-series labels

Often you will be charting a worksheet where the data does not allow you to easily include the legends or X-series labels (e.g. the column headings may be on two rows as in this example or the X-series labels may not be included when you highlight the data).

Open the file PRAC2 and create a column chart using the data in cells **B4** to **D9** (ignoring the title, column headings and totals for now).

Start the **Chart Wizard** and select **Column** chart type. On the second screen click on the **Series** button and you will see the following.

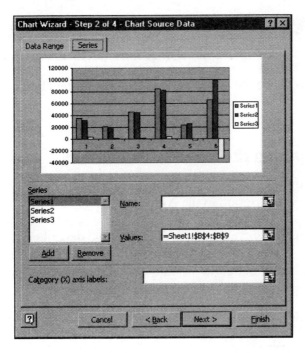

At present, there are no **Category (X) axis labels** and the legends are not very helpful.

Changing the X-series labels

Click on the button at the end of the **Category (X) axis labels** box.

This will return you to the worksheet, highlight the names of the people and then click on the (end) button of the dialog box to return to the chart.

You will see the X-series labels appear in the chart.

Changing the legend descriptions

Highlight each series (Series1, etc.) in turn and type the correct description in the **Name** box.

Alternatively, you can use the technique described above.

Click on the button at the end of the **Name** box and highlight the required data in the worksheet, e.g.

This is how the **Chart Wizard** dialog box should look at this stage.

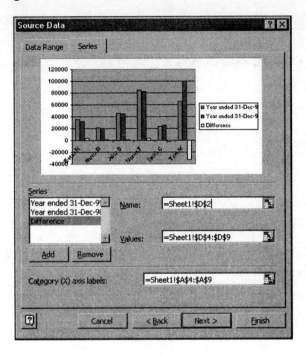

Carry on with the **Wizard** adding the necessary data. At this stage it will look similar to this.

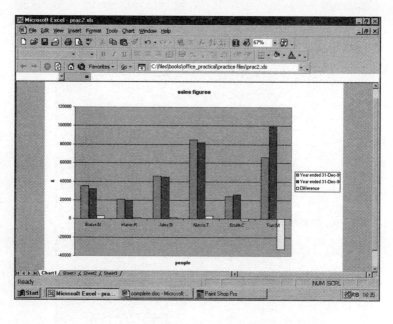

134

Altering the position of the X-series labels

Click the X-axis (be careful to be precise where you click) and you should see this dialog box. Make sure you are looking at the **Patterns** dialog box.

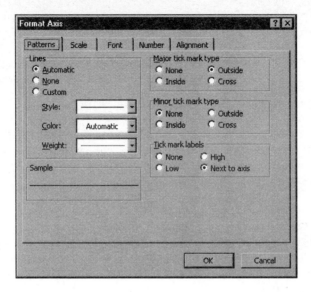

Ensure that you have selected **Low** for **Tick mark labels** and see the result. This avoids the labels getting in the way of the columns.

Apply the following formatting:

❑ Format the title to a larger size.

❑ Place a shadowed border around the whole chart (double-click the edge of the chart to display the dialog box).

❑ Alter the look of the columns so that it is easy to distinguish between them when printed in black and white.

❑ Enter your name as a header.

❑ Enter the file name and date as footers.

❑ Preview the file and if it looks satisfactory, print it out.

Here is my version.

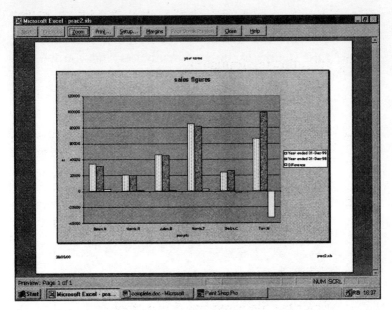

Save the file.

Altering the Y-axis scale

Double click the Y-axis to display the **Format Axis** dialog box and select the **Scale** tab, alter the **Maximum** and **Minor unit** figures to those shown below and you will see how the chart has changed.

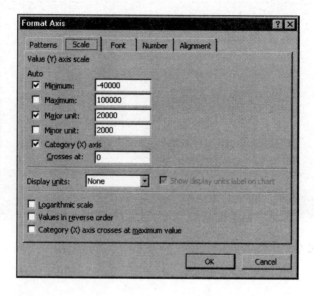

The bars in the chart fill more of the chart area.

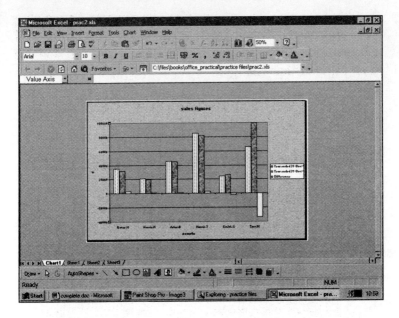

Save the file.

Reorganising the series order

You can change the order of the series, i.e. the sequence in which the data is shown in the chart.

To do this, select any of the data series (bars in the chart) and pull down the **Format** menu and select **Selected Data Series**. You will see the following dialog box if you select the **Series Order** tab.

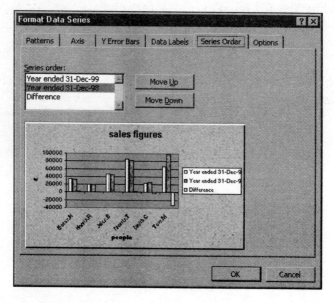

You can then alter the order by moving any of the data series up or down.

Try this to see the effect.

Close the file without saving the changes you have just made.

Practice

Open PRAC4 and create a column chart (excluding the **Percentage Reduction** column and the **Totals**, but including the **Sale Price** column) i.e. include cells **A2:B6** and **D2:E6**

> You can select the data you want to include by highlighting the data in the first row or column and then holding the **CTRL** key down and clicking and dragging the mouse to highlight the remainder of the data (which need not be in consecutive rows or columns).

Use your imagination to produce a professional looking result.

Adding text boxes and arrows

You are going to add a text box with suitable text to show the most expensive pet. To do this, you need to use the **Drawing** toolbar (**View** menu, **Toolbars**, **Drawing**).

Click on the **Text Box** button, click, and drag the mouse to create a text box. Enter the text you want (altering the font, resizing the box and so on as necessary).

Click on the **arrow** button to draw an arrow (if you then double-click the arrow you can alter the way it looks). Here is an example of how the final version could look.

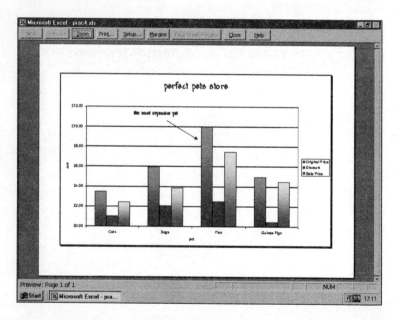

Save and close the worksheet.

Pie Charts

Pie charts are a popular way of illustrating data although they can only be used for one series of data (per chart).

Open the file PRAC1, highlight the cells A2 to B5, and start the **Chart Wizard**.

Choose the **Pie** and move onto **step 3** of the wizard. At this point, click the **Data Labels** tab and select **Show label and percent**. Ensure (in **step 4**) that you select **As New Chart** and you will see the pie chart displayed.

Alter the chart (font, colours and so on) to make it look professional and easy to understand. My version is shown below.

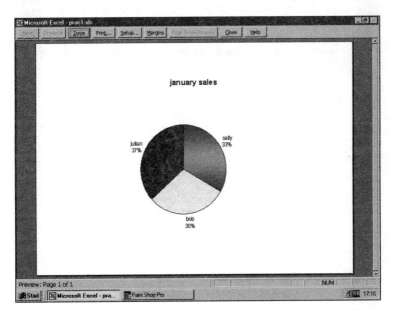

To practise this, create a pie chart for the month of March (remember to only highlight A2:A5 and D2:D5).

Here is my version.

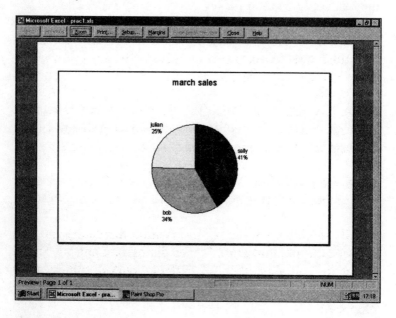

Save and close the file.

Pictograms

This type of chart can be very effective to illustrate data.

To begin you need to have created a column chart, to practise open PRAC1 and view the worksheet you created. Pull down the **Insert** menu and select **Picture** followed by **Clip Art**. Choose a picture.

Select the picture and then click the **Copy** button, switch to the (column) chart and select any of the columns (make sure that all the columns for the same series are selected).

Click the **Paste** button and you will see a picture replacing the original column.

Finally double-click the picture (within the chart) and you will see the **Format Data Series** dialog box appear. Select **Patterns** and then the **Fill Effects** button followed by **Format**, **Stack and Scale**, click **OK** until the chart reappears.

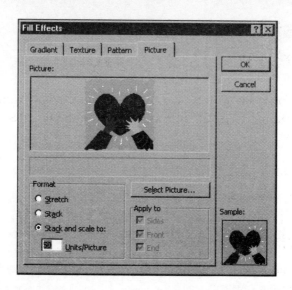

Repeat this process for each data series.

The results should look similar to this.

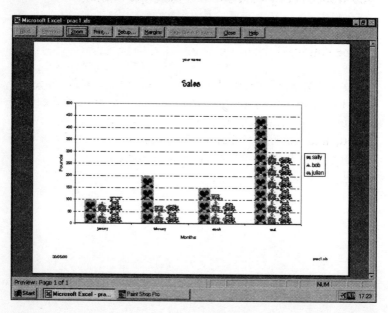

Pasting charts and worksheets into Word

It is likely that you will want to put charts and worksheet data you have created in Excel in Word documents, e.g. in a report.

You can do this in stages:

Worksheets (data)

Open your Word document and then minimise the Word screen.

Open the Excel file and highlight the data in the worksheet you want to copy then click on the **copy** button.

Switch to the Word document and position the cursor where you want the worksheet data to appear.

Click the **paste** button, the data is pasted as a Word table, and this can be formatted as desired, e.g. you can centre the table by clicking within it, pulling down the **Table** menu, and selecting **Table Properties**. Select the **Table** tab and then **Center**, this centres the table.

Charts

Open your Word document and then minimise the Word screen.

Open the Excel file and select the worksheet you want to copy, click on the **copy** button.

Switch to the Word document and position the cursor where you want the chart to appear.

Pull down the **Edit** menu and select **Paste Special**, select **Picture** from the list and then **OK**.

If you want to centre the chart, then **right click** it and select **Format Picture** followed by **Layout**. Choose **In line with text (Wrapping style)** and then use the **Center** button on the toolbar to centre the chart on the page.

Linking the Word and Excel files

You can link the spreadsheet or chart you have pasted into Word so that when you make changes to the original Excel file, the changes will automatically be reflected in the Word file.

To achieve this, you must use **Paste Special** and click the **Paste link** button.

With charts, you should paste them as **Microsoft Excel Chart Object** (you may have to alter the size to fit the page).

Practice

Create a new word document and copy the worksheet and chart from the exercise PRAC1. The results should look similar to this.

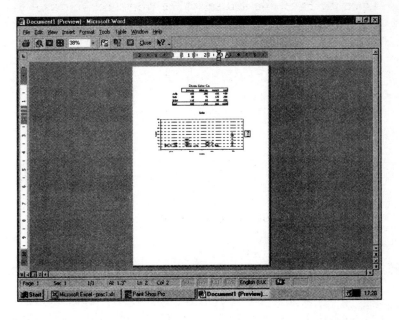

PowerPoint

Starting off

After loading the program, you will then see the dialog box shown below.

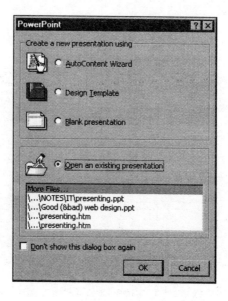

Creating a new presentation

If necessary, select **Blank presentation** by clicking the mouse so that a dot appears in front of the words and then click on **OK**.

You should see the following:

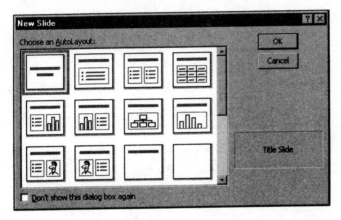

If not already selected, click on the very first **AutoLayout** and then on **OK**.

You will see the title screen.

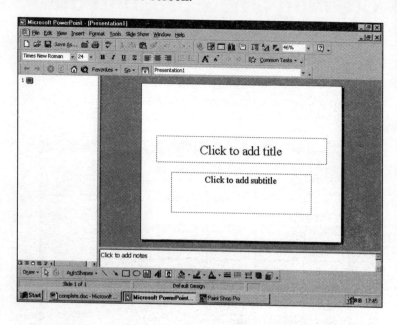

I suggest you drag the divider to the left, giving yourself a larger area in which to work.

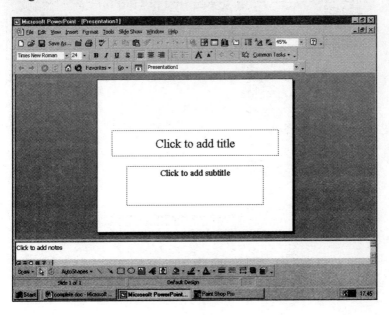

Entering Text

Make the window full-screen by clicking on the appropriate button (if it is not already full-screen).

Enter the following title (click the mouse within the existing text to begin).

My First Slide Show

Enter the following subtitle:

Using PowerPoint

Click on the **New Slide** button (top toolbar).

Select the second **AutoLayout** and you should see the following screen.

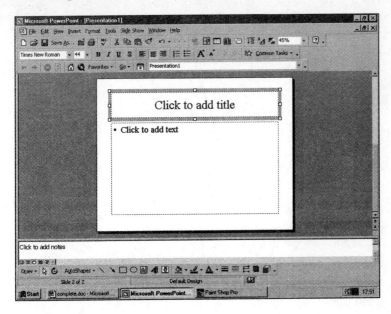

Add the following title:

The First Slide

Add the text:

Line One

Press the **return** key and then enter the following lines, pressing **return** between each:

Line Two

Line Three

Line Four

Click on the **New Slide** button and again choose the second layout.

Add the following title:

The Second Slide

Add the text (exactly as spelt).

Line Fiive

Line Siix

Line Sevenn

Line Ate

Line Nine

You have now created three slides.

Saving your work

It is best to save your work regularly. To do so click on the **Save** button (upper toolbar), click in the **File name** box and name your file PRESENT1. Save it to the folder of your choice.

Text editing

Use the double-headed arrows on the bottom right of the screen to move back to the initial slide (titled **My First Slide Show**).

To alter the font, highlight the text by clicking and dragging the mouse, then click on the arrow to the right of each of the toolbar buttons (shown below) to pull down the choices and then scroll up or down the list until you get to your choice.

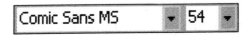

Alter the title font to **Comic Sans 54 pt** and the subtitle to the same font and **44 pt** size.

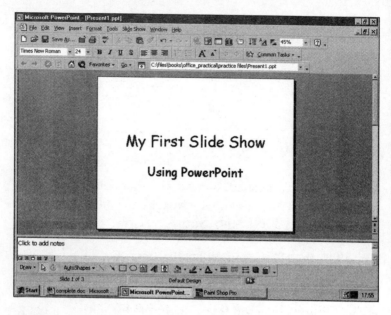

Use the double-arrow buttons to move to the next slide (titled **The First Slide**).

Now you are going to alter the size of the title (of this slide) to **Comic Sans 54 pt** and the text to **Times New Roman 44 pt**.

Move to the final slide and alter the fonts in the same way.

Move back to the slide titled **The First Slide**.

Select the text (by highlighting) and pull down the **Format**
menu and then **Line Spacing**.

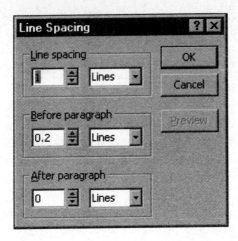

Alter the **Before Paragraph** to **0.5** and then click on the
Preview button, if satisfactory click on **OK**.

Make sure all the text is still selected and then
use the **Center** button on the toolbar to centre
the text (note that this centres each line between
the margins).

Move to the final slide and again highlight the text.

From the **Format** menu select **Bullets and Numbering**,
then **Character** and select **Wingdings** from the **Bullets
from** list, choose a new bullet, then alter the various
options (**Color, Size** and so on), and finally click on **OK**.

Do this again, this time choosing a sensible bullet.

You now need to use the **Drawing** toolbar, this should be displayed along the bottom of the screen, however if it is not then pull down the **View** menu, select **Toolbars** and then **Drawing**. The toolbar looks like this.

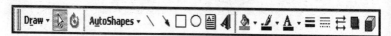

Make sure the text is still highlighted and then use the **Font Color** button on the **Drawing** toolbar to colour the text **Blue** (you may need to click on the arrow to the right of the button and then select **More Font Colors**).

Now just highlight the word **Sevenn** and change its colour to **Black**.

Move back to the first slide (titled **My First Slide Show**) and select the subtitle by clicking to display the text border.

From the **Draw** menu (**Drawing** toolbar), choose **Rotate or Flip** and then **Free Rotate**. Grab one of the corners of the text border and rotate the text.

Alternatively, you could also use the rotate button to the right of the **Draw** menu.

Grab the text and drag it further down the slide.

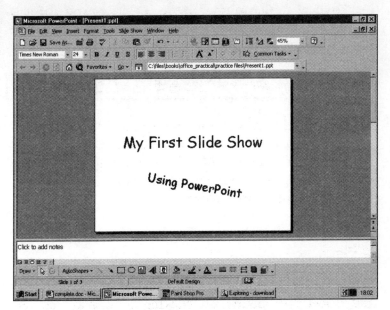

Finally click on the **Spelling** button and spell check your slides, correcting as necessary.

The spelling dialog box is shown below.

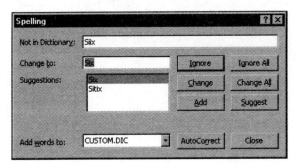

You have various options; you can **Ignore** or **Ignore All** (occurrences of the word), **Change** to the correct spelling or **Add** to the dictionary.

Remember that the spellchecker may identify a word that is correct but not within its dictionary. The spell check did not pick up the word **Ate** in the final slide. You will need to alter this manually.

Save the file.

Transitions

So far, you have produced a series of three slides. Now you are going to see how they look as a slide show, using the transition effect (this alters the way in which each slide is loaded onto the screen).

Click on the **Slide Sorter View** button (bottom left of the screen).

You will see all the slides together.

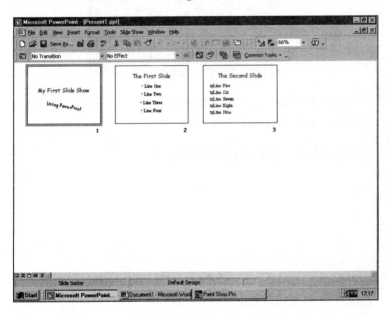

Pull down the **Edit** menu and choose **Select All**.

Use the **Slide Transition** button to create a transition, you can see the effects displayed as you choose the different transitions.

165

Alternatively, pull down the **Slide Show** menu and select **Slide Transition**.

You can alter the speed of the transition and add sounds. I suggest you begin with the **Slow**.

Finally, click on the **Apply to All** button.

Animations

With all the slides selected, you can apply special effects to the way in which the lines of text are displayed.

To use this click on the arrow to the right of the **Preset Animation** box, this is displayed on the toolbar to the right of the Transitions button.

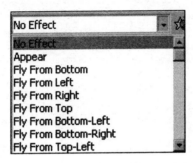

Select the animation you want to use.

Now, click on the **Slide Show** button along the bottom left of the screen and use the left-hand mouse button to advance the text and slides.

Practise altering the **Transition** and **Animations**, so you can see the effect of the different techniques.

Looking at your Slides

Slide Sorter

You have already used this to produce transitions and animations for the slide show, another use is to rearrange the slides.

> The next technique will not work if the slides are all still selected; if they are still all selected, click the cursor away from them.

Click on the **Slide Sorter** button. You will see all the slides together. Now grab the last slide with the mouse and drag it in front of the first slide (you will see a line appear where the slide will be moved to).

Move it back.

Use the **Normal View** button to return to the slides.

Printing the slides

You can print your slides one to a page onto paper or you can print them onto transparencies directly using a colour ink-jet printer.

You can print the slides (up to) six to a page so you can issue them as handouts to your audience.

To print, pull down the **File** menu, select **Print,** and select the options you require, the illustration shows the options for printing six to a page.

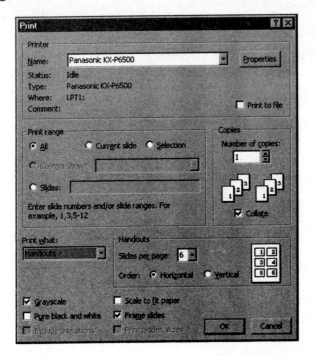

Save the file.

If you want to save the file under a different name or to a different directory, you need to pull down the **File** menu and then choose **Save As**.

Slide Designs

You can add a background design to your slides (and this is normally recommended) by clicking on the **Common Tasks** button and selecting **Apply Design Template**.

You should see a list of designs with a small illustration to the right of the selected design.

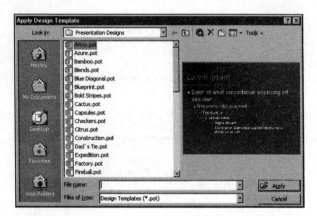

Choose the design you want to apply by scrolling down the list using the cursor keys to move down the list. Click on **Apply** to add the chosen design.

If you are to apply a design then it is best to apply it at the start of the creation of your slide show, since it may alter any existing fonts and layout.

If you want to change the design simply repeat the process.

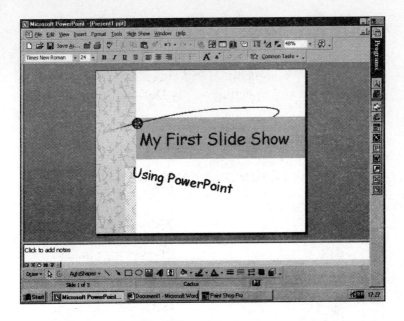

Save and close the file (**File**, **Close**).

Adding Graphics

The fun starts. **Used sensibly**, graphics add to a presentation.

Start a new file (click on the **New File** button on the left of the upper toolbar). Then choose the blank **AutoLayout** (bottom right of the choices).

Clipart

Then pull down the **Insert** menu, **Picture** and then **Clip Art**.

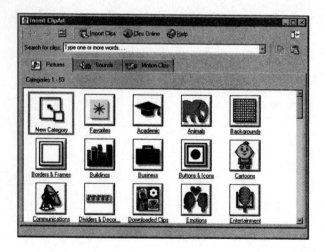

Choose a picture. Click on **Insert**.

The picture will appear within the slide. Do not worry about its size or position at present.

WordArt

Create a second slide (**New Slide** button) and select the blank **Auto Layout**.

Select the **Insert WordArt** button from the **Drawing** toolbar (if it is not shown, pull down the **View** menu, select **Toolbars** followed by **Drawing**).

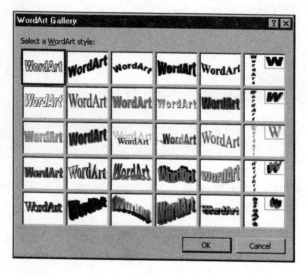

Choose a format and click **OK**.

Enter the following text (by overtyping the original text) and click the **OK** button.

Fancy Letters

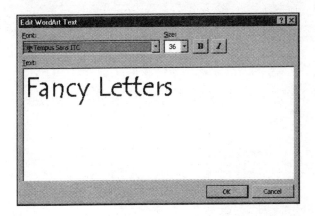

Remember if you want to alter it afterwards click the mouse on the text and **Word Art** toolbar will be loaded automatically and you can use the various buttons to create effects.

Your finished slide may look like this.

Save the file as PRESENT2.

You can also access **Word Art** from the **Insert** menu, followed by **Object** and from the list **Microsoft WordArt 3.2**

Organisation Charts

Click on the **New Slide** button and then select the **Organisation Chart** AutoLayout.

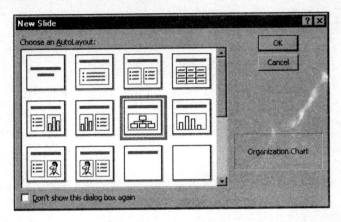

Once the slide has appeared, double-click the organisation chart button and the module will (eventually) appear.

Make the window full screen.

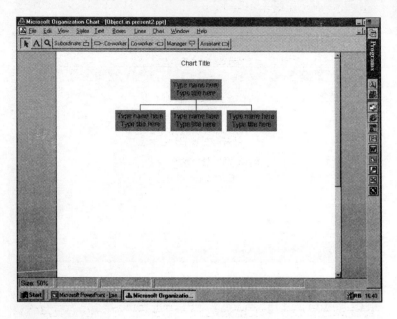

Click on the box to the far right and delete it (use the **Delete** key).

Click on the **Subordinate** button and then on the box to the left. This will add the subordinate below that box.

Subordinate: 🔲

Now add a **Co-worker** box to the side of the **Subordinate** box.

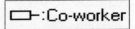

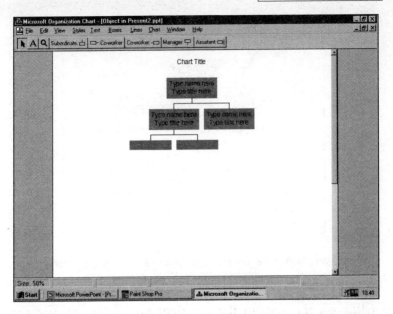

Pull down the **Edit** menu, **Select Levels**, and then **Levels 1 to 3**.

Pull down the **Boxes** menu and select the **Color**, then colour the boxes **white**.

In a similar way, colour the borders of the boxes **red** (**Boxes**, **Border Color**).

Pull down the **Text** menu and select **Color**, make sure that **black** is selected.

Finally, pull down the **Chart** menu and alter the **Background Color** to **light gray**.

179

Add the following text by overtyping the existing text by clicking within each box, typing, and then clicking outside each box when finished.

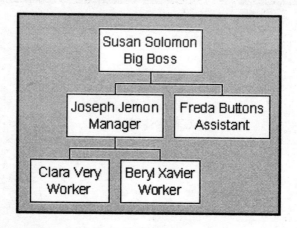

Pull down the **File** menu and then **Exit and return** (and **Yes** to any question that appears).

If you want to make any changes, double-click the chart to load the organisation chart module.

Click in the title area and enter the title:

Swansong Company PLC

Alter the font to Tahoma 44 pt.

You have created your own customised organisation chart, do not worry about its size or position at present.

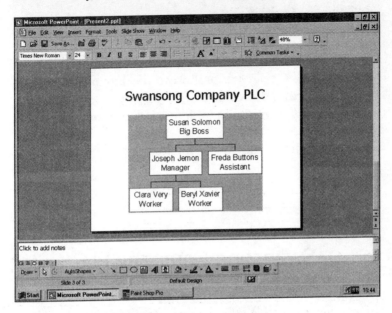

Finally, save your new file as PRESENT2.

Borders/Arrows

On the last slide containing the organisation chart. Scale the chart to (say) 70% (**right-click** the chart, select **Format Object** and the **Size**).

Drag the picture to the centre of the slide.

Use the **Insert Clip Art** button to insert a picture, choose a suitable image for Susan.

Scale this to a suitable size and move it to the right of the box for Susan Solomon.

Now click on the **Arrow** button and draw an arrow from the picture to Susan.

With the arrow selected, pull down the **Format** menu and then **Colors and Lines** and alter the line colour and style of the arrow (or you can double-click the arrow).

Now add a picture and arrow for Joseph (the manager).

The result may look similar to this.

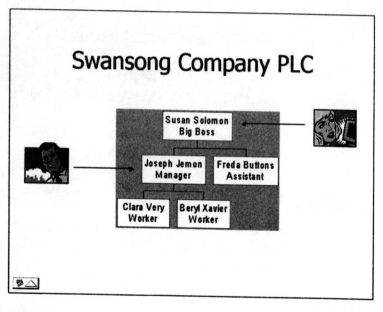

Finally, save the file.

Adding sounds (and movies)

You can add sounds and movies to your slides, though this can make the slide show slower to display.

Move back to the very first slide, move the picture into the bottom two-thirds of the slide.

Pull down the **Format** menu and **Slide Layout**. Select the **Title Only** (**AutoLayout**), this will impose a title area on to the slide.

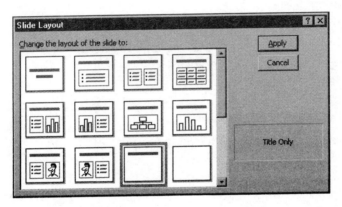

Add the following title:

Sounds and movies too!

Pull down the **Insert** menu and then **Movies and Sounds** followed by **Sounds from Gallery**. Select a sound, it will appear within the slide as a speaker icon.

You will be given a choice as to whether the sound starts automatically or not.

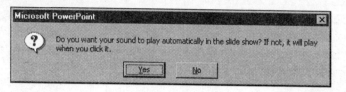

You can also **right-click** the icon (selecting **Edit Sound Object**) and make it keep looping (this may become irritating).

I have enlarged it in the illustration below so you can see it clearly.

When you run your slide show you can click the icon with the mouse and you will hear the sound.

Movies work in a similar way.

Save and close the file.

Altering Slides

Making changes on the master slide will affect all the slides making up the presentation.

Open the first file you created (PRESENT1), using the **Open** button to do so.

Master Slides

Click on the **View** menu and then **Master** and finally **Slide Master**. The master will appear.

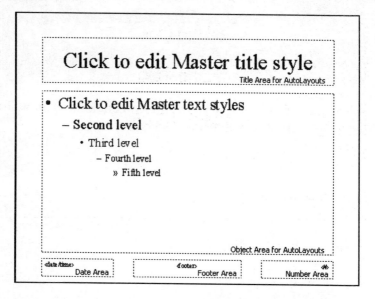

Anything you add to the master slide will appear on every slide in the slide show (of that layout type, altering the slide master will not make any changes to the title master).

Highlight the *<date/time>* and pull down the **Insert** menu and select **Date and Time,** choose one of these, note the **Update automatically** button.

Highlight the *<footer>* and enter your name.

Return to the slides by clicking on the **Slide View** button and go to the initial slide. Now click on the **Slide Show** button to display your slides with the time/date and your name shown on each.

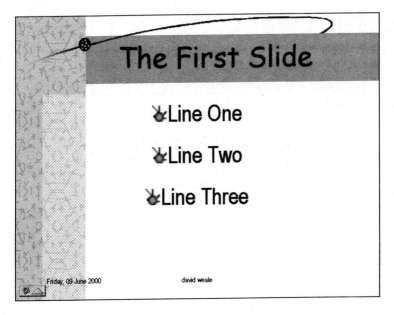

Save and close the file.

Running slide shows automatically

Self-running presentations are useful for exhibitions and displays, as they do not need anyone to be physically present. A self-running presentation can be set to loop repeatedly.

To set up a self-running show: open a presentation, select the **Slide Show** menu, followed by **Set Up Show**.

Click **Browsed at a kiosk (full screen)**, this automatically selects the **Loop continuously until 'Esc'** option.

The **Using timings, if present** option is also set.

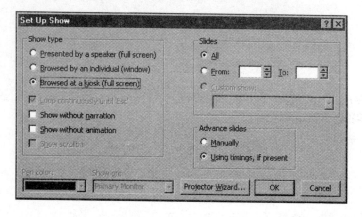

Setting timings

Pull down the **Slide Show** menu. Select **Slide Transition** and then alter the settings as desired so that the slides advance after a certain number of seconds.

You can also use the **Rehearse Timings** option on the **Slide Show** menu.

Use the **Next** button (the first button on the **Rehearsal** toolbar shown above) to decide how long you want the viewer to see each point. You can then save the timings and they will be used when the slide show is run.

You can add recorded narration to your slide show by using the **Record Narration** option in the **Slide Show** menu.

Access

What is a database

Databases are used to store information, for example customer or employee names and details. The data can be looked at (interrogated) in different ways, e.g. all the customers within a postal area could be printed out. The data can be added to, edited, deleted, and viewed in various ways (forms, reports, etc).

The structure

A data file is made up of records, there being as many records as there are items in the database (e.g. every employee would have their own record within the database).

A record is made up of fields; a field has two parts, the field name, and the data in that field. A record will have several fields, each containing a different type of data.

field	data
Surname	Adams
Christian name	Sarah
D.O.B.	01/6/54
Email	Saraha@cara.net

An individual record

Database programs are available in different levels of complexity and sophistication.

Flat-form databases

These are similar to the traditional card index file. The ways in which data can be looked at varies with the sophistication of the program (and of the user). Usually you can look at the data using multiple fields (e.g. all those employees aged over 50 earning more than £15000); the data can be sorted into any order. It can be printed or displayed on the screen.

Relational databases

These are a more complex version of a database. More than one database file can be opened at one time and the files can be manipulated together.

For example, for security purposes, a firm may decide to have two data files for the employees, one a personnel file (each record containing names, ages, home address, etc.) and the other a salary file (each record containing names and salary details).

These operate as separate data files, but in a relational structure they can be linked (if needed) by a common field e.g. the name field.

Thus an authorised person could look at both data files together and would be able to look at both salary details and personnel data (something other employees could not do), and could manipulate data across both files, e.g. add new data, create new fields, etc., which would update both databases.

Beginnings

When you start up Access, you will see the following screen.

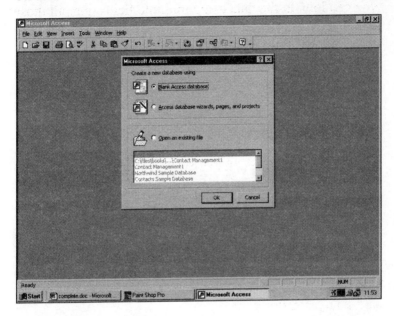

Choose **Blank Access Database**.

Next, you will be asked to save the file (call it PEOPLE).

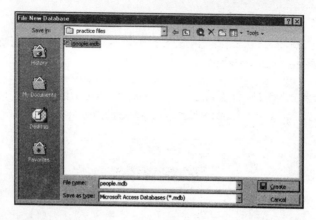

The next screen asks you to choose the method you want to use to create the structure of the database.

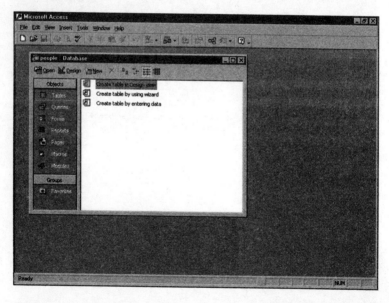

Choose the first option **Create table in Design view** and click the **Design** button (or double-click the option).

Tables are used to store the data, every other activity uses the table as the data source.

You can now decide upon the names and data type for the fields in your database.

To alter the **Data Type** from text, click on the arrow to the right and select from the pull down menu.

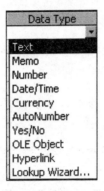

Enter the following details, using the **tab** key to move to the next item.

Field Name	Data Type
Company Name	Text
Address 1	Text
Address 2	Text
Town / Village	Text
County	Text
Postcode	Text
Date entered	Date/Time
Credit Limit	Currency

Close this down and save the table, giving it the name **Customer Details**.

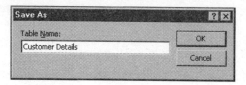

You will be asked if you want to create a primary key (this is the field used to organise the database).

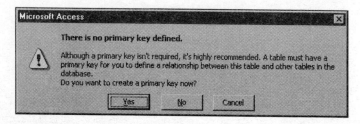

Click on the **Yes** button and you should see the screen shown below.

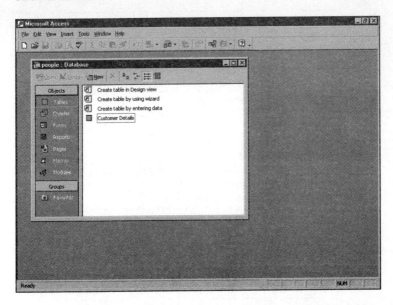

Select **Customer Details** and click the **Open** button, enter the following data (the **ID** is entered automatically by the program).

Use the **tab** key to move onto the next field.

You must enter the / symbol in the date field (as shown below).

ID	1	2	3	4
Company Name	Fantastic Foods	Lickable Ices	Smashing Salads	Better Bakes
Address 1	The Old Mill	Station Road	Sunnyside	12 Dreadnought Avenue
Address 2	Brook Lane		Jonah Close	
Town/ Village	Yeovilton	Ilminster	Exeter	Exmouth
County	Somerset	Somerset	Devon	Devon
Postcode	BA65 8TR	TA2 6YU	EX5 9EW	EX7 4WS
Date entered	24/12/97	13/01/98	12/12/97	14/02/96
Credit Limit	£5,000.00	£7,000.00	£3,000.00	£8,000.00

Check the data for accuracy.

Finally, close all the files, saving any changes.

Adding data to a database

Open the file PEOPLE and then the table **Customer Details**.

Click on the next record and enter the following data.

ID	5	6
Company Name	Delightful Donuts	Exciting Edibles
Address 1	Unit 4	87b High Street
Address 2	Spring Park	
Town / Village	Plymouth	Midsomer Norton
County	Devon	Somerset
Postcode	PL6 8TR	TA45 7R
Date entered	23/05/94	13/06/95
Credit Limit	£2000	£3500

If the display does not show all the data in each field then you can alter the width manually, move the mouse pointer to the divide between two column letters when it will become a two-arrowhead cross.

Click and drag the divider until you are happy.

You can also alter the width by highlighting the column(s) and pulling down the **Format** menu and selecting **Column Width** (you might like to select **Best Fit**).

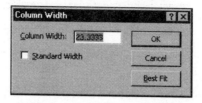

Alternatively, you can make the text smaller by pulling down the **Format** menu and then **Font**.

Sorting the data

Pull down the **Records** menu; select **Filter** followed by **Advanced Filter/Sort**. You will see a new screen.

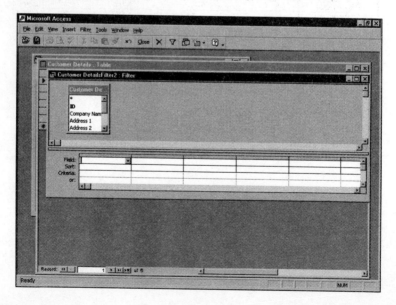

Enter the following details for **Field** and **Sort** by clicking in the box and then on the arrow symbol to the right of the box, selecting the data shown below.

Field:	County ▾	Company Name
Sort:	Ascending	Ascending
Criteria:		
or:		
	◄ ■	

Pull down the **Filter** menu and then **Apply Filter/Sort**, the data should be sorted by County and **within** County by Company Name, i.e. the Counties are in order (Devon first) and within Devon the company names are in order of company.

ID	Company Name	Address 1	Address 2	Town/Village	County	Postcode	Date entered	Credit Limit
4	Better Bakes	12 Dreadnought Avenue		Exmouth	Devon	EX7 4WS	14/02/96	£8,000.00
5	Delightful Donuts	Unit 4	Spring Park	Plymouth	Devon	PL8 8TR	23/05/94	£2,000.00
3	Smashing Salads	Sunnyside	Jonah Close	Exeter	Devon	EX5 9EW	12/12/97	£3,000.00
6	Exciting Edibles	87b High Street		Midsomer Norton	Somerset	TA45 7R	13/06/95	£3,500.00
1	Fantastic Foods	The Old Mill	Brook Lane	Yeovilton	Somerset	BA65 8TR	24/12/97	£5,000.00
2	Lickable Ices	Station Road		Ilminster	Somerset	TA2 6YU	13/01/98	£7,000.00

Applying Filters

A filter lets you choose which parts of the database to display.

Pull down the **Records** menu; select **Filter** followed by **Advanced Filter/Sort**.

Type the word **Devon** in the **Criteria** under **County**, then pull down the **Filter** menu, and select **Apply Filter/Sort**.

Your database should now only display the companies in Devon.

ID	Company Name	Address 1	Address 2	Town/Village	County	Postcode	Date entered	Credit Limit
1	Better Bakes	12 Dreadnought Avenue		Exmouth	Devon	EX7 4WS	14/02/96	£8,000.00
5	Delightful Donuts	Unit 4	Spring Park	Plymouth	Devon	PL8 8TR	23/05/94	£2,000.00
3	Smashing Salads	Sunnyside	Jonah Close	Exeter	Devon	EX5 9EW	12/12/97	£3,000.00

Finally, pull down the **Records** menu and then **Remove Filter/Sort**. Your data should be back in its original state.

Close and (if prompted) save all the open files.

Forms

You can create a form for a variety of purposes, for example as a data entry form.

Open the PEOPLE file, click on **Forms** and then **New**.

Choose the **Form Wizard** and **Customer Details** as the table or query.

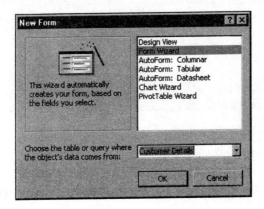

On the next screen, click on the symbol to
include all the fields in the form.

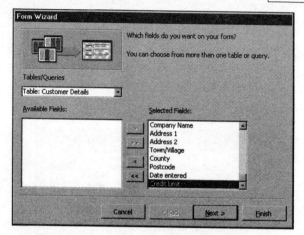

Carry on, choosing **Columnar** and then **Blends** on the next
two screens.

Click on **Finish** and you will see the form displayed on the
screen.

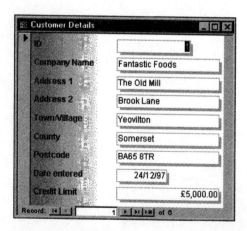

Maximise the window and you have a data entry screen, which looks rather more professional than the **Datasheet** you used to enter the original data.

Click on the symbol at the bottom of the window to enter a new record and then enter the data shown below.

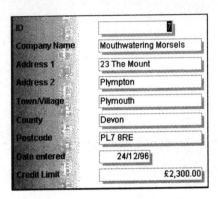

Now close down this window and return to the original window.

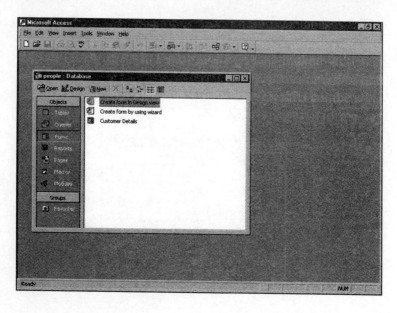

Reports

From this screen, select **Reports**.

Choose the **Create report by using wizard**, followed by **New**.

Select **Report Wizard** and **Customer Details** as the table or query.

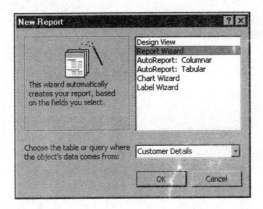

Choose to enter all the fields into the report
except for the **ID** and **Date entered** fields (use
the single arrow button to enter each field).

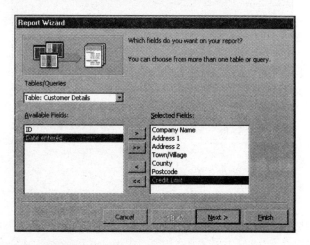

On the next screen, group by **County** and then by **Credit
Limit** by selecting the fields and clicking on the arrow.

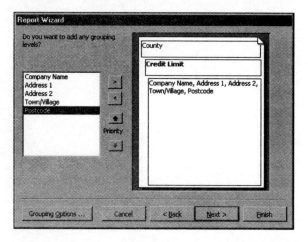

On the next screen, choose to sort by **Company Name**.

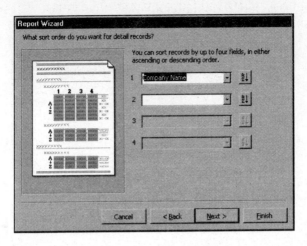

On the next screen, choose **Landscape** (orientation) and **Stepped** layout and from the following screen **Soft Gray** style. Finally, click on **Finish** and you will see the report previewed on the screen.

Pull down the **View** menu, **Zoom** and **Fit to Window**. You will see the report as shown below.

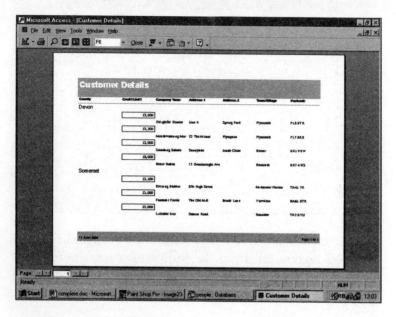

Unfortunately, all the data is not displayed (for example some of the Company Names are not shown in full).

Close this screen.

Customising the report layout

Click the **Design** button. You will see the design of the report.

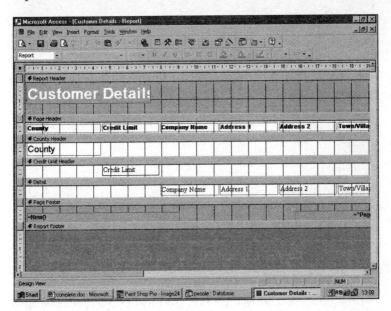

Increase the size of the **Detail** area by clicking and dragging the bottom of the area, then click, and drag the bottom of the **Company Name** and **Address 1** boxes to make them bigger (the end result is shown below).

Close down the **Design View** window, saving the changes.

Make sure that the **Customer Details** report is highlighted.

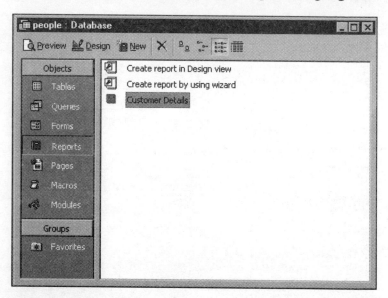

Click on the **Preview** button and pull down the **View** menu, **Zoom** and **Fit to Window**. You will see the report with all the data shown (if not, go through the process until it is).

Finally, close down all the open windows and close the file.

Practice

Open the PEOPLE database file and create a new **Table** (**Table** followed by **Create table in Design view**).

The table should have fields and field types as shown below.

Field Name	Data Type
Company Name	Text
First Name	Text
Last Name	Text
Phone	Text
Email	Text

Set the **Primary Key** after clicking in the **Company Name** field (**Edit** followed by **Primary Key**), and close the window, saving and calling the table **Contacts**.

Create a **New Form** (use the **Form Wizard**) using the **Contacts** table, include all the fields and whatever design features you want.

Use the form to enter the following data.

Company Name	First Name	Last Name	Phone	Email
Better Bakes	Julie	Harris	01935-65-3452	julieh@bb-net.com
Delightful Donuts	Donald	Dougan	0187-345654	donald.dougan@virginal.net
Exciting Edibles	Boris	Baskerville	0198-34-2345	boris.b@claris.net
Fantastic Foods	Cyril	Rakins	01786-761292	c.rakins@fast.net
Lickable Ices	Harry	Andrews	01543-65784	harryandrews@lices.com
Mouthwatering Morsels	Sally	Dodgy	0171-547865	sally.d@virginal.net
Smashing Salads	Fiona	Fortescue	01327-45632	fiona.fort@demons.net

Close the form.

Relationships between tables

You have now created two tables, **Customer Details** and **Contacts**. There is a common field (**Customer Name**) in each of the tables.

Creating the relationship

You should be looking at the following screen.

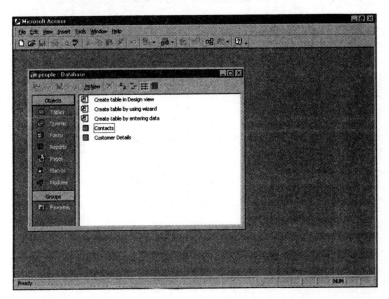

Now click on the **Relationships** button on the toolbar.

The following will appear.

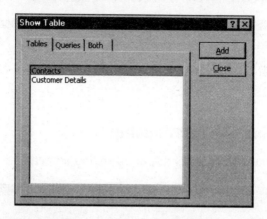

Click on each and then on the **Add** button (press the **Ctrl** key while clicking the **Add** button to select both) then click the **Close** button.

You should see the **Relationships** screen.

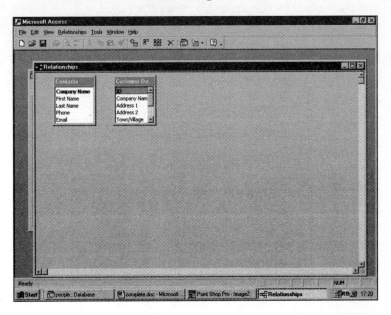

Click on the **Company Name** field in the **Customer Details** box and drag it to the **Company Name** in the **Contacts** box.

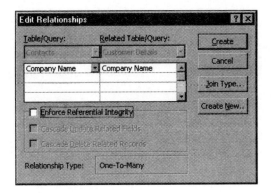

It is very important that the data is as shown above, if it is not then click on the arrows to alter the fields.

Click the **Create** button.

You should now see an arrow joining the two boxes; this means there is a relationship between them.

If you want to delete a relationship, press the **Delete** key.

Close down the **Relationships** window (saving the changes).

Queries

These are similar in nature to **Filters/Sort** with the difference that **Queries** can be used to look at data in related tables and Queries can be saved and reused.

Click on **Queries** and double-click **Create query in Design view**.

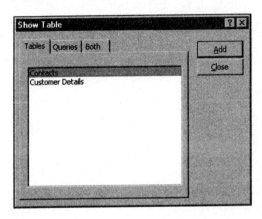

Select the **Contacts** table, then **Add**, finally **Close**.

Enter the fields shown below into the query (you can drag them from the list or pull down the arrows and select from the list).

Field:	Company Name	First Name	Last Name	Email
Table:	Contacts	Contacts	Contacts	Contacts
Sort:				
Show:	☑	☑	☑	☑
Criteria:				
or:				

Click on the **Show Table** button on the toolbar and **Add** the **Customer Details** table, then close the dialog box.

Add the **Credit Limit** field (this is the last field in the table) and **Sort** this (Descending).

Field:	Company Name	First Name	Last Name	Email	Credit Limit
Table:	Contacts	Contacts	Contacts	Contacts	Customer Details
Sort:					Descending
Show:	☑	☑	☑	☑	☑
Criteria:					
or:					

Finally click on the **Run** button on the toolbar (to run the query) and you should see the following data.

Company Name	First Name	Last Name	Email	Credit Limit
Better Bakes	Julie	Harris	julie@bb.net	£8,000.00
Lickable Ices	Harry	Andrews	harryandrews@lices.com	£7,000.00
Fantastic Foods	Cyril	Rakins	c.rakins@fast.net	£5,000.00
Exciting Edibles	Boris	Baskerville	boris@claris.net	£3,500.00
Smashing Salads	Fiona	Fortescue	fiona.fort@demons.net	£3,000.00
Mouthwatering Morsels	Sally	Dodgy	sally.d@virginal.net	£2,300.00
Delightful Donuts	Donald	Dougan	donald.dougan@virginal.net	£2,000.00

Finally, close down the query screens (saving the query as **Query1**).

Creating a report from a query

Once you have run a query you can create a report from the data contained therein.

To do so, click on the **Reports** and then **New**. Select **Report Wizard** and choose **Query1** as the table/query.

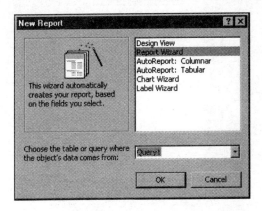

Make your choices and you will end up with something similar to this.

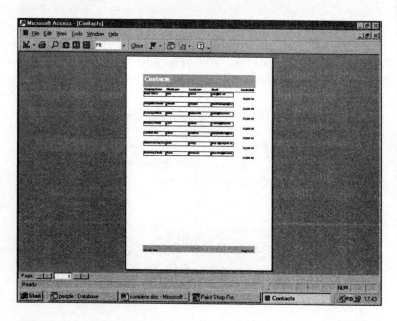

Close down the report windows and save the report as **Contacts**.

Extracting data from a database

You can use **Filters** or **Queries** to extract data from a database.

These can be used in a more sophisticated way than has already been covered; e.g., you can include criteria within the query.

Select **Queries** and then **Create query by using wizard**.

Include the fields shown below from the **Contacts** and **Customer Details** tables, selecting each in turn from the **Tables/Queries** box (pull down the list using the arrow to the right).

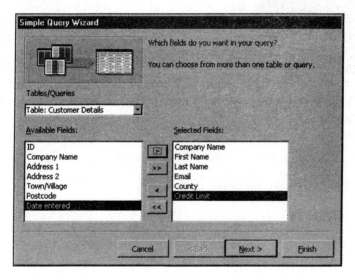

Accept the defaults for the rest of the screens and you should see the following result.

Company Name	First Name	Last Name	Email	County	Credit Limit
Better Bakes	Julie	Harris	julie@bb.net	Devon	£8,000.00
Delightful Donuts	Donald	Dougan	donald.dougan@virginal.net	Devon	£2,000.00
Exciting Edibles	Boris	Baskerville	boris@claris.net	Somerset	£3,500.00
Fantastic Foods	Cyril	Rakins	c.rakins@fast.net	Somerset	£5,000.00
Lickable Ices	Harry	Andrews	harryandrews@lices.com	Somerset	£7,000.00
Mouthwatering Morsels	Sally	Dodgy	sally.d@virginal.net	Devon	£2,300.00
Smashing Salads	Fiona	Fortescue	fiona.fort@demons.net	Devon	£3,000.00

Now pull down the **Records** menu and select **Filter**, then **Advanced Filter/Sort**.

Enter the following data.

Field:	County	Credit Limit
Sort:		
Criteria:	"Devon"	>2100
or:		

Finally, pull down the **Filter** menu and select **Apply Filter/Sort** and you will see the following.

Company Name	First Name	Last Name	Email	County	Credit Limit
Smashing Salads	Fiona	Fortescue	fiona.fort@demons.net	Devon	£3,000.00
Better Bakes	Julie	Harris	julie@bb.net	Devon	£8,000.00
Mouthwatering Morsels	Sally	Dodgy	sally.d@virginal.net	Devon	£2,300.00

Close down the window, saving it.

Finally, to create a report based upon the filtered data and including a calculation:

Click on the **Reports** and then on **Create report by using wizard**.

Use the **Reports Wizard** and choose **Contacts Query** as the table/query to be used for the report.

Include all the fields.

Accept the next screens and then choose to sort by **Credit Limit**.

Choose **Landscape** orientation otherwise accept the defaults. The result should look like this.

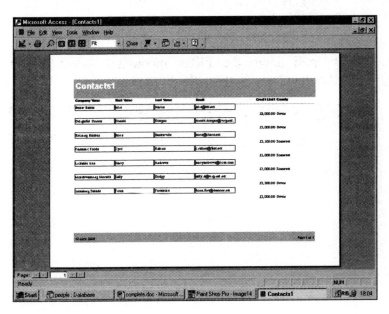

Close all the files and exit the program.

Appendices

The Standard Buttons

Microsoft Windows 98 lets you alter the size of the active window; there are four buttons, which appear on every window.

Clicking on this button closes down the program (you will be asked if you want to save any changes that you have made to the file).

This reduces the size of the window to its previous size. This button is an alternative to the next one.

This button enlarges the active (current) window to fill the screen.

This button minimises the window, if you do this you will see the program name appearing along the Windows 98 **Start** bar at the bottom of the screen. You can click on the program name to activate it.

Help

All Windows programs feature on-line **Help** that is valuable and easy to use, and makes both learning and problem solving easier.

All the programs have a **Help** pull down menu (Access has been used as an example but all the applications are similar).

The Office Assistant

The assistant is normally always on screen or can be called from the menu by selecting **Microsoft (Access) Help**.

To get help double-click your assistant and you will see a dialog box where you ask your question.

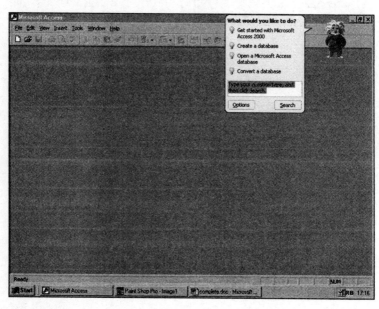

The Options button

Click the **Options** button and you can choose a new assistant by clicking the **Gallery** tab or make changes to the default settings.

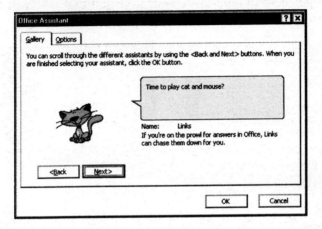

The Search button

You type in a query and click the **Search** button. The results will be displayed; you then select which answer is closest and click this, finally arriving at the actual help screen on the right of the screen.

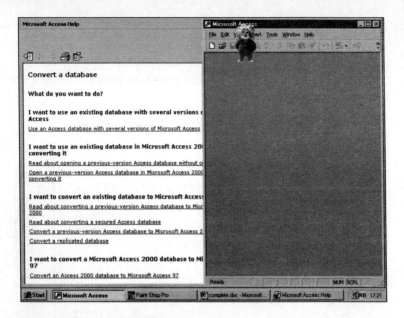

You can move around the help screens by clicking the hyperlinks (which are underlined and normally in blue).

Note the buttons along the top of the help screen; the first of these is the **Show** button used to display the more traditional method of obtaining help.

The other buttons enable you to move back or forward through the screens you have looked at or to print out the text. There is an **Options** button on the far right which adds certain features.

234

Using the Show button

As you can see from the illustration, you have the **Contents**, **Answer Wizard** and **Index** options.

Contents

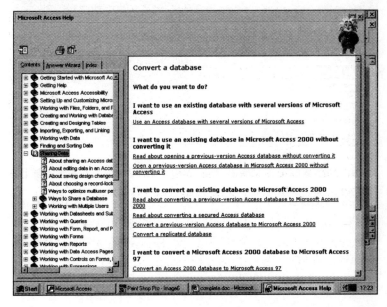

As you can see from the picture, the contents are like a series of books or chapters on the various aspects of the program.

Each book can be opened by double-clicking on it to reveal the sections within that book.

Answer Wizard

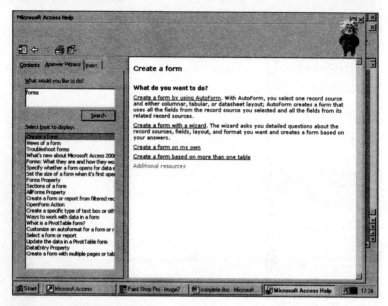

Instead of choosing from a list, here you type in the word or phrase and the nearest equivalents are displayed so you can select the one you want. The details are then shown in the right pane.

Index

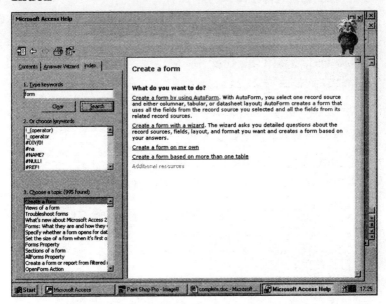

This includes a list of keywords as well as the option of typing a keyword.

Office on the Web

This option will connect you to the Microsoft site on the Internet. Your browser (e.g. Microsoft Explorer) will be loaded and so will the site.

Detect and Repair

This option will, with the help of the original discs, fix problems in the installation of the program.

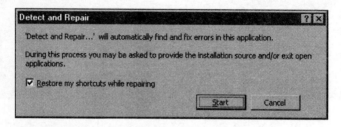

About Microsoft (Access)

This displays information about the program.

Index

A

Absolute reference 117
Align Right 10, 77
Alignment 48, 100, 126, 127
Animation 167
Answer Wizard 235
Assistant..232, 233
AutoLayout.....................................153, 157, 172, 174, 177, 183
AutoSum...79, 92, 104

B

Blank presentation 153
Break..17, 45, 58
Bullets 7, 31, 32, 161

C

Categories 70
Chart title 123, 126
Chart type 121, 125, 131
Chart Wizard....................................120, 125, 131, 133
Clip Art...34, 172, 181
Custom border 128
Custom header 87
Customise 32, 40
Cut 7, 20

D

Data form 66
Data type 197
Database 194
Database Wizard 195
Datasheet 207
Design view 213, 215
Details 236
Drawing 142, 162

E

Edit 33, 66, 125, 165, 179, 215
Effects 128, 145, 165, 167, 175
Explorer 238

F

Field 65, 67, 203
Fill 38, 77, 128, 139, 145, 230
Filter 202, 203, 204, 226, 227
Find 33
Fit to 86, 94, 101, 105, 212, 214
Flat-form 194
Flip 162
Font size 14, 82
Footer 27, 28, 29, 60, 61, 63, 87, 187
Footnote 42, 43
Free rotate 162
Freezing panes 119
Function key 44, 61, 118
Functions 104

G

Gallery 34, 183, 233
Grid...47, 49, 112
Group 210

H

Header.............................27, 60, 87, 94, 101, 105, 129, 136
Height 34, 100

I

Inches...25
Indent...7, 25
Index 58, 235, 237
Internet...238

J

Justify...10, 12

K

Kiosk...188

L

Line spacing...16, 161
List...236, 237
Lookup...114, 115

M

Mail merge...64, 68
Margins...40, 62, 63, 87, 161
Master slide...186
Measurement units...25
Merge..64, 67, 68, 81

N

New slide...156, 158, 174, 177
Normal view..2
Numbering...31, 32, 161

O

Organisation chart...177, 180, 181
Orientation.......................40, 41, 94, 101, 105, 127, 211, 227
Orphans...18
Outline..83

P

Page break...17, 45, 58
Page setup...40, 51, 86
Paper size...40
Pattern...22, 23, 50
Pivot table...110, 112, 113
Portrait...40, 41
Primary key...198, 215

Q

Query 221, 225, 227
Query wizard 225

R

Record....................................189, 193, 194, 201, 207
Relational...194
Replace 33
Report Wizard...209
Reports...................................192, 209, 223, 227
Rotate...162
Row..100
Run.....................................185, 189, 222, 223

S

Save as 5, 31, 32, 36, 46, 97, 169
Scale......................................138, 145, 181, 182
Search 33, 233
Section break 45
Shading..............7, 22, 23, 47, 51, 83, 94, 101, 105
Slide Sorter 165, 168
Spelling..3, 19, 163, 164
Standard buttons 230
Start bar...230
Styles 54 56, 62
Symbol.........................29, 32, 47, 91, 199, 203, 206, 207

T

Table of contents 54, 58
Tables 47, 58, 197
Template 62, 63, 170
Text box 142
Tick mark labels 136
Transition 165, 166, 167, 189

U

Undo 15, 127
Update 56, 61, 187, 194

W

Web 238
Widows 18
Wingdings 32, 161
Word Art 37, 38, 74, 175
Word count 39
Wrap 35, 100

X

X-series 131, 132, 135

Z

Zoom 9, 212, 214